HAPPINESS

One Day at a Time

Collective

HAPPINESS

Modus Vivendi Publishing Inc.

© 1998 Modus Vivendi Publishing Inc.

Published by:
Modus Vivendi Publishing Inc.
2565, Broadway, Suite 281
New-York, NY 10025

Cover design and illustrations: Marc Alain
Page layout: Modus Vivendi Publishing Inc.

ISBN 2-921556-54-5

Foreword

The Simplicity of Things

*T*oday, we are getting back to basics. When the intellectuals, theologians and philosophers took control of "Truth", life became extremely complicated. These thinkers told us that it was impossible to know and to prosper without following in their footsteps. Realize that by accepting their path, we are accepting the truth of others. It is preferable by far to listen to one's self, to listen to my our wisdom. Our own wisdom cannot lie, it belongs to us. When we listen to ourselves, things become much simpler.

We can be aware of the truths that have always served us well and we can make optimal use of them. Based on these truths, we can also build our own moral code and our own value system. By living honestly, by bringing integrity, justice and wisdom into our lives, we can live in harmony and prosperity. *Happiness — One Day at a Time* looks at ethics, wisdom and truth. But ethics, wisdom and truth cannot be borrowed from others. Rather, through our experiences, our relationships with others and in the profound sense of awareness that exists in all of us, we can discover our own form of ethics, wisdom and truth.

Introduction

*T*here are laws. Moral principles govern our lives, here on earth, as we interact with other human beings. With every fiber of our beings, we seek to create beauty and harmony in our own lives and in the lives of others. We strive to achieve this objective naturally, given our fundamental nature.

But in our feverish race to achieve material success, the approval of others and financial security, we sometimes neglect to identify and adhere to the fundamental principles that contribute to happiness and beauty.

We can trust our ability to make the right choices and to become the ultimate masters of our destiny. By listening to ourselves and by applying our own rules of behavior, we succeed in rising above the depths of the superficial world of appearances, toward true life and self-determination and the enormous rewards they entail.

By applying certain fundamental life principles, we can live in harmony with the forces that govern the earth and the universe in general. By living in harmony with our principles, we embrace the strength of truth and simplicity and encounter much fewer experiences of resistance and defeat. As you read through this book, you will be amazed at the simplicity of the principles that take the shape of affirmations and very personal realizations. May they guide you on your personal path to love, joy and serenity. Bon voyage!

Being

"Being happy and satisfied doesn't mean doing or accomplishing something: we need to be, not do."
— SHARON WEGSCHEIDER-CRUSE

Now I understand the difference between doing and being. I don't need to do something to be someone. Being, in itself, is enough. Appropriate actions will follow naturally. I have realized that I can't buy love or loyalty. I can't allow myself to do a series of things with the sole purpose of earning appreciation or being loved. All I have to do is recognize and experience being.

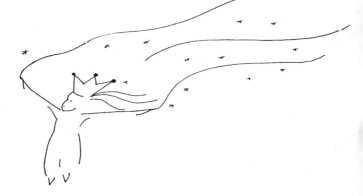

Being Myself

I can be myself at all times and under all circumstances. The people around me and those like me are always very happy to see who I really am. Being myself requires no special effort. Being myself is being spontaneous, expressing myself fully, not holding back. When I am myself, I can experience people and things directly. I can be truly present.

I have learned to look at change and improvement as a process that lets me learn to know who I am. The fundamental being that I am is absolutely wonderful. As I grow, I shed all the layers which hide the true me.

Respecting My Individuality

I've realized that I am totally unique and totally different from the other beings who share this planet with
me. No, I am not a small particle of cosmic energy. I
am a complete and self-reliant being. I am capable of
expressing opinions, making decisions, creating
things, taking action. I am completely self-reliant and
I decide my own fate.

I know that above all else, I am a spiritual being that
exists beyond my physical body. I am a spirit, a luminous and powerful being living in a borrowed body.
It's that simple. But if I spend my life giving into and
worshipping my body and other material things, I'll
miss the boat. I will succeed only in shrinking away
and losing my real power. Of course, I must respect
my physical body and I must maintain it properly, but
I cannot be a slave to it.

I Am a Child of the Universe

"You are a child of the universe, just as the trees and the stars are: you have the right to be here. And whether or not it is clear to you, there is no doubt that the universe is unfolding as it should."

— MAX EHRMANN

Today, I take the place that belongs to me because I realize that I have a right to be here and to enjoy the things and the events in my life. I have the right to be here, in contact with those close to me. I want to be seen and I want to be heard. I can make things happen and I can even make mistakes. I have a right to do all these things.

My Divine Nature

"All of us are here to go beyond our initial limitations, whatever they may be. We are here to recognize our magnificent and divine nature, regardless of what it may tell us."

— LOUISE HAY

Now I accept the fact that I am here to grow, to love and to learn. I am not here to accumulate material wealth, to win over others or to plan my retirement. I am here to contribute to my self-fulfillment and the fulfillment of others.

My Inner Knowledge

Over time, I've learned that I must put all my focus on inner knowledge. I've realized that the greatest truth is what I come to know through my experiences, my senses and my intelligence. There is no more vital or more obvious truth than the knowledge that comes from within me. I know that I must listen to my inner self, to my feelings and to my perceptions. This way, I will always be faithful to myself and to my principles.

My Road

I know that I am an individual being and so my road is my road, my thoughts are my thoughts and my actions are my actions. By recognizing and respecting my own individuality, I give power to my decisions and my actions. My individuality is also a great responsibility: I am responsible for my own happiness and my own growth.

I am completely happy with my individuality and I accept the challenge and the responsibility of travelling my own road. I know that by putting "me" first and by choosing to follow my own road and my inner knowledge, I will always live well and I will never lack essentials. Throughout life, we encounter advice and ideas of every imaginable kind. I listen to others, but I know that before all else, I must listen to myself and to my own ideas. The more I develop my ability to listen, the more faithful I am to myself. Today, I am travelling my own road.

Making My Place in the World

Now I see the world around me. A world filled with life and movement. I look around me and I see the world with a certain detachment. I look around me from a distance so that I can be in the best position to see, to take in, to understand life and the beings living on this planet. In this way, I am able to build a better place in this fascinating world.

Choice

"Someday, your heart will tell you what to do."
— ACHAAN CHAH

Today, I'll take the time to make choices based on my own needs and the needs that result from specific situations. Because of my past, sometime I let myself be overwhelmed by the demands and needs of others. In the past, I have made hasty choices which later had an effect on my life. Now I know that I can say "yes", "no", "maybe" or "I can't decide right now". I give myself the luxury of choosing at my own pace. Today, I choose to listen to myself.

From now on, I consider my choices intelligent and important. I take the time to make the choices that are right for me and I am proud of myself. I trust myself and my focus is choosing wisely, without haste.

Learning to Think for Myself

I have realized that my most precious asset in life is knowing how to think for myself and trying to understand things and people. I respect my ability to learn, to think freely and to know.

In the past, learning was something frightening and unknown to me. I also believed that what I really thought was not important. Today, I realize how important what I think really is and I know that I am unique and creative. When I think for myself, I assert my independence and my ability to be who I am.

Enjoying My Freedom

I am a free being. I am free to explore, to take risks, to be spontaneous and to do what I need to do. Freedom of choice and freedom of action means that I must be completely faithful to myself and to my principles.

My freedom is expressed through my imagination, my ability to make choices and my freedom of expression and action.

Liking Who I Am

"When you really love yourself, when you approve of yourself and when you accept yourself as you are, everything goes well in life. It's as if small miracles come into your life every day."

— LOUISE HAY

I like the person I am and the person I am becoming. I have all the talents and attributes to succeed. I congratulate myself for being the wonderful person I am. Today, I continue to move away from the enemies who don't want me to love myself. There are many enemies of this kind and they take various forms: negative comments, people who question my personal integrity and encourage me to become too dependent on others. I have found the right tools to reinforce my self-worth: work, communication, exercise, acknowledgment of my feelings, affirmation of my needs and personal limits that are clear to others. I don't need to do anything special to be likeable or to be loved. I am worthy of receiving and giving love. I can love myself because I am and because every living being deserves to be loved.

Accepting Myself Unconditionally

"Gradually I must accept myself as I am — with no secrets, no disguises, no falseness and no rejection of any facet of myself — and with no judgement, no condemnation or denigration of any facet of myself."
— ANONYMOUS

There came a time in my life when I could no longer live for others or for the approval of others. There came a time when I understood that I had to accept myself as I was and that I had to love myself if I wanted to grow.

When I accept myself as I am, I can live happily. When I take myself by the hand and welcome myself to the human race, I can be happy. I am a valuable human being. I can love myself. I can spoil myself. I can give myself permission to live, to laugh and to have fun. I can have things that contribute to my well-being and my self-fulfillment. I can learn, grow and change. I deserve a life filled with love, joy and pleasure. I deserve good friends who cherish me and who want me to be happy. I deserve recognition, respect and admiration. I am a very valuable person.

All the Beautiful Things in Life

I see how I have set limits on what I can or cannot have. For a long time, I lived with a profound feeling of lack. This attitude of not being able to have one thing or another, one relationship or another, only served to destroy my ability to have and to keep. Today, I give myself the permission to have. I let things and relationships come to me.

Learning from My Mistakes

I have forgiven myself for mistakes made in the past. What is past is past. So, I say goodbye to past mistakes.

I know that I am here to learn, to grow and to experience life. So I accept that mistakes are a part of life. When I make a mistake, I use it to learn and to adjust my aim. Now I accept the fact that mistakes are on the road I travel.

Living Each Experience

Today, I am open to all experiences. I am ready to live through each one of them. I know that I have nothing to fear and nothing to run away from and I know that I can trust myself completely. I also know that the areas of life and the experiences I choose to resist have a hold on me and wear me down. Today, I have decided to stop running away and to face all the experiences and all the different aspects of my life.

Now I can face all of my feelings. I have learned that the feelings I resist end up ruling and upsetting me even more. I am capable of having feelings and of expressing them freely when I am among friends. When I try to stop the natural flow of my emotions, I imprison their energy within me. So I have decided to set my emotions free.

Where Does Despair Come From?

"Our preoccupations should lead us to action, not depression."

— KAREN HORNEY

Too many people are depressed when they consider today's issues. It may be true that there is a lot to do to make this world a better place. But contributing to making it better is a at least a step in the right direction, one step closer to the final goal. Our actions often have a powerful effect on others. Today, I have decided to take action to change all I can possibly change, for the better.

Being Here, Right Now

"Yesterday no longer exists. Tomorrow may never come. The miracle of the present moment is all there is. Enjoy it. It is a gift."

— MARIE STILKIND

I enjoy being here, right now. I have had to go through difficult stages, but now I try to be prepared to take on adversity and all other situations calmly and intelligently. I am in control of my life and my fate. Today, I announce the start of a wonderful new adventure.

I now realize that the past is nothing else but the past. I take hold of the present moment and I have the ability to see and to imagine my future. This vision lets me shape and create an ideal place for myself in the world.

The Power of My Dreams

Today, I give myself permission to dream and I try to make my dreams come true. When I was much younger, I had all sorts of projects and all sorts of goals. I used to imagine my life and my future and I used to be fed by my dreams. It seems to me that I could see myself growing up and reaching my goals and my ability to dream helped me build and choose. And most importantly, the ability to dream enabled me to rise above the boredom and dullness of daily life. But gradually, my dreams faded and I stopped using my ability to dream. Now I know that the moment I stopped dreaming, I stopped living and enjoying the creative experience life brings.

Today, I nourish my dreams. Today, I let my imagination run wild and I see my ideal future materialize before my very eyes. My ability to create dreams gives me hope and inspiration in my daily life. Today, I dream and I try to make my dreams come true.

The Magic of Silence

I have always thought that there was some kind of magic in silence. Silence is alive and active. Silence shows me all the things that are possible, all that I cannot hear in the noise of everyday life. My heart and my soul look for the silence they need to express themselves, to speak to me. In moments of tranquillity and silence, I find calmness and courage. So each day, I look for small moments of silence.

At the end of a very active day, I set aside a few moments. Sometimes I pray and sometimes I take the time to think, nothing more. Today, I give myself moments of silence and I enjoy them because I know that in such moments, I come into closest contact with myself.

The Space Between You and Me

There is a distance, a space between you and me. I am me and you are you. I have my viewpoints, my opinions and my desires and they are different from yours. I have the right to be who I am, to have my own way of thinking and to live my own emotions and you have the same rights. I respect the fact that you make your own choices. You must also accept that I am free to make my own decisions.

I have learned that love and sharing are possible only when we respect the other's boundaries and when we affirm our own. When I build a safe space around me, I can live more peacefully, without fear and without confusion. So today, I can distinguish between who I am and who you are.

The Consequences of My Actions

The actions I take have consequences and I am aware of this fact. Just as the actions of those around me can affect me, I realize that my own behaviours have repercussions on those around me. Being conscious of my actions is important and crucial. This lets me realize how a small joke can affect the people I love and how important it is to take positive actions in my life.

What I say and what I do can affect those around me. I must identify the motivations that lead me to say certain things and to do certain things. By identifying what motivates me to act in a specific way, I can improve the quality of my relationships.

Today I choose to open my eyes, my heart and my mind. Today, I recognize that each of my actions is important. I resolve to remain aware of how my actions can affect others.

Here to Love and to Learn

Deep down I have the feeling that I am here to love and to learn. This is the core of my mission on earth. I know that I can accomplish my fundamental mission in many ways.

Each day, I must keep an open mind so that I can learn new lessons. I must share what I have learned in such a way that I can help others. I must contribute to the well-being and happiness of the people around me. I am not a saint, but I am aware of my own mission of loving and learning.

Today, I know that my life has a meaning. The meaning is found in the mission of loving and learning, every single day.

My Individuality

I can state that:

- I am completely different from anyone else;
- I have qualities found only in me;
- I make my own decisions.

I accept my deep individuality. When I was younger, I felt that there was a difference between me and other people. Sometimes I liked my individuality, and sometimes it upset me. But with time, I realized that my individuality found its source in something very deep within me. I am myself, and I am perfect as I am. Individuality is what makes life interesting and colorful. Today, I accept my individuality and the individuality of others.

Finding My Inner Child

There is more and more talk about finding one's inner child. For me, this means making contact with the person I really am. As I grow older, I know that my looks have changed and that I have a few more wrinkles. But I know the difference between what is me and what is nothing like me. Finding the child in me means being spontaneous, present and authentic. Today, I let others see the real me, the child within.

Being Faithful to Myself

"Faithfulness is the only currency that keeps its value over time."

— FRANÇOIS GARAGNON

Faithfulness is a very noble value. Being faithful in a love or business relationship proves our maturity and our worth as a friend or associate. When we are faithful and when we show that we deserve to be trusted, we can build solid relationships that can stand the test of time.

But before being faithful to others, we must be faithful to ourselves, to our values, to our principles and to our own experience. Being faithful to ourselves means recognizing our right to choose. It means recognizing and learning from our mistakes and rewarding ourselves for the good things we do. Being faithful to ourselves means listening to ourselves and to our hearts. It means having the courage of our convictions and the strength to make choices and to accept our individuality. Today, I am faithful to myself.

Positive Thinking

I didn't always believe that thoughts could have an influence on my life. I believed that positive thinking was a way to hide or cover up the truth. If things were going wrong, things were going wrong — it was beyond my control. But I discovered that my way of seeing things had a definite influence on my life experiences. There is something basic that comes before action and experience and that something is my attitude.

Today, I have a positive attitude. I have the attitude of a winner. I tell myself that despite difficulties and stumbling blocks, I can succeed. I have all the tools, all the talents and all the courage I need to succeed. I can change a defeat into a victory.

A Generous Heart

"If a blind man helped a cripple to walk, the two could go far."

— SWEDISH PROVERB

Goodness has nothing to do with the fear of not being loved. Goodness stems from a generous heart. I do not show that I am good so that everyone can see, for I am naturally good.

Being good and loving others is another way of expressing my true self. I am a good and generous person. Today, I need only listen to my inner self to know what is right. I am willing to lend a hand to others and I am happy that I can help them.

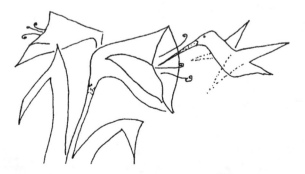

Pleasure

"Today, it seems that periodically, we have an inborn need to change the state of our consciousness: through our daydreams, the things that make us laugh, the sports we practise, the projects we focus on, or the simple fact of sleeping the time away. Another modified state of mind and a another deep-rooted need is also linked to this process: experiencing pleasure and having fun. Many children from dysfunctional families have a hard time relaxing and having fun. The ability to be spontaneous and to have fun is a need and a characteristic of the Inner Child."

— CHARLES L. WHITFIELD

For a long time I believed that I had to be serious and I also believed that there was a spiritual side to suffering. It seems that I established a relationship between belief and suffering. Suffering was a synonym for nobleness. But eventually, I realized that suffering did not necessarily change me and more importantly, that it did not necessarily bring me more happiness or peace of mind. Today, I am open to all experiences and I welcome joy and pleasure. I look for opportunities to share happiness and joy-giving experiences.

Games

My life had become a constant fight for survival. I felt that most people were against me and were intentionally or unconsciously trying to keep me from growing. There was no real joy in my life, only a few minutes of peace here and there. My road in life was a hard one to travel. I felt trapped.

I have come to understand that games and fun are a part of life. I give myself the right to have fun. Today, I see life as a game that offers many different opportunities and possibilities and I choose those I want to experience.

Hiding Behind Defeat

Behind each "no" is a "yes". Behind each defeat is a victory. We can learn much more from our failures than we can from our successes. Hidden behind each failure is everything that we haven't understood, everything we haven't wanted to accept, everything we haven't wanted to see or hear. When I welcome failure and when I'm ready to hear the secrets it wants to tell me, I am open to growth and to learning. Today, I know that eventually, a defeat can become a great victory. Defeat keeps me on my toes and it helps me to go farther than I ever thought I could. When faced with defeat, my reaction is curiosity, not discouragement.

The Power of Truth

"... as long as there is a distinction between what should be and what is, conflicts will occur systematically, and all sources of conflict are a waste of energy."
— KRISHANAMURTI

There is one sure value in this universe: the power of truth. Truth constantly strives to show itself. It exists in everything around us. Gradually, I am beginning to see it. Either in my relationships or in things that concern me directly, I put truth at the head of my list of values. I know that truth is synonymous with freedom. When I am truthful, I am free.

Today, I make truth my top priority. I see things as they are and I face up to truth. I am honest with myself and others and I am proud of myself for being able to be so.

Seeing Things as They Are

I understand that I must see things as they are. I am setting out to handle difficulties head-on, to solve problems and to see clearly. When I see things clearly, I can act logically until the situation I am in ends, in the way I want it to end. By confronting obstacles directly, I become stronger and less dependent on my environment and the various situations I encounter in life. The fears I may have felt in the past fade quickly in the light of reality. Looking things as they are lets me consider every angle and lets me make the right decisions.

Today, I am no longer stubborn and I've stopped trying to impose my opinions on others. I simply see life as it is. Just as darkness always gives way to light, truth wins over lies and deception.

What Is Obvious

"Peace comes only to one who seeks. Peace comes only to one who finds."

— Raoul Duguay

Sometimes, I get upset because I've forgotten simply to look at what is in front of me. I have created illusions by believing what I've heard instead of looking myself, to see what was really there. How many times have I made myself unhappy by listening to others instead of using my own awareness.

Now I realize something that is very important; I have decided to look and to see for myself.

Letting Go Doesn't Mean Quitting

Today, I tell myself that life can be something like a dance. If I have clear intentions and an ability to adapt, I can reach my goals. For me, letting go means letting go of the idea that I can control anything or avoid anything. And it means accepting that I have a flexible and intelligent control over things and events. So instead of trying to exercise complete control and use brute force, I try to fall in step with the flow of events. Today, I play and I dance with the various situations I encounter in my life.

The Answer Is Within Me

"Always look inside yourself for the answer. Do not let yourself be influenced by those around you, nor by their thoughts or their words..."

— EILEEN CADDY

Now I look inside myself for the answers to the important questions in my life. No one can give me better advice than my inner self because my inner self knows exactly where I am, who I am and where I am going. Each individual has his or her own opinions and experiences and when they give me advice, sometimes they can show me the path to follow. Nevertheless, I am responsible for my own fate and my own life and I must accept fully that I am my own guide throughout the path that is my life.

Honesty

I include honesty in my everyday life. With time, I have come to understand that being frank with myself and with others is crucial to my happiness and my success. It is important that I be honest with myself and that I communicate directly with my relatives, friends and associates. Honesty is a great source of pleasure for me. Each time I am honest with myself and others, I feel a great sense of value and respect for myself.

Today, I know the difference between truth and lies. I choose to live honestly and frankly.

Courage

I am courageous and I recognize that courage is the key to growth and change. When we seek to go beyond our own limitations, to break down life's barriers, we are immediately faced with the fear and humiliation of failure. But what sense of victory or joy can there be for anyone afraid to dare? I feel a great sense of courage as I head into the future because I know that I can rely on myself. I also know that a life without risk is not really a life at all. It is better to die standing than to have lived a life on one's knees.

The Real Source of Problems

When I recognize the power of truth, I can always identify the true source of problems. In reality, a problem is only something that I cannot or will not face. A problem is something I refuse to confront. I cannot control what I choose to avoid or what I choose to resist.

By understanding the fundamental nature of a problem, I can solve it. I have the ability to find solutions to the problems I am experiencing. I take the time I need to consider the solutions available to me. Then I take action to settle the situation.

I work to identify the real sources of my problems and my troubles. With time, I have realized that if a difficult problem or situation persists, the reason is that I have not found its source. All I have to do is look carefully and truly listen to the truth. Eventually, I will be able to find the true causes to problems.

The Light Within

"What we create within ourselves is always reflected on the outside. Such is the law of the universe."
— SHAKTI GAWAIN

We live in an upside down world. Appearances are what counts: a person's age, his or her state of health, how big their home is, the model and year of their automobile. In reality, these things are not very important. At the most, they can indicate that a person has succeeded materially or he or she is in good physical shape (which is nothing wrong in itself). However, if we have all the material wealth and all the physical beauty we could ever wish for, but we are not truly happy and deeply satisfied, we are living in a state of degradation. Today, I am investing in my awakening and my growth as a spiritual being because I know that I am valuable.

What I Chase After

When I chase after something relentlessly, without looking at its true nature, I tend to make that something run away from me. Instead of imposing, I should be receptive and I should wait for the right moment.

Time is malleable. My chance will come soon, so why should I be impatient? I make my decision and I wait for the right time and… it comes! If I know that I'm lacking something or that something is out of my reach, I imagine the result I want, I make my decision and then I take action.

Being Right at All Costs

Today, more and more I avoid the type of situation where I feel I must be right at all costs. When I find myself in this kind of situation of conflict, I know there is something I am unable to admit. So I have to back away from the situation to see more clearly what it is I am refusing to face.

Today, I know that I can be right and I can be wrong. I don't need to be right at all costs. I can let things go. If I want to, I can let the other person be right. Today, I have the flexibility of being right or being wrong. Ultimately, I recognize that I can win a battle but lose the war. So I look at each situation carefully and I don't let myself be overwhelmed by the need to be right at all costs.

Being Sincere

*"To thine own self be true
And it shall follow, as the night the day
Thou canst not then be false to any man."*
— WILLIAM SHAKESPEARE

I am faithful to my principles, to my ideals and to my dreams. I know what I have to do to feel good about myself. At every moment and in every situation, I apply simple rules of behavior — rules that have always served me well. I am cordial, honest and fair with myself and with others. I know that to be happy, I must develop open and satisfying relationships with the people around me. I can be patient and loving toward others, even when they do things that I don't like. I understand that life isn't always easy. I refuse to plunge into anger, jealously or hatred because I know that none of these emotions are part of my true nature.

Admitting My Faults

I must be honest with myself. I must be able to admit my faults. Admitting my faults does not mean "feeling guilty". Instead, it means taking responsibility for the feelings I've caused and admitting that I did what I did. That's all I have to do.

I have the ability to admit my faults, my mistakes and the harm I have caused. I know that I'm not always right and I can be mistaken at times. By keeping an open mind when it comes to the opinions of other people, by being able to see things from different perspectives, I can understand other people more easily and I can accept their viewpoints. By being able to understand and accept others points of view, I can more easily adapt my actions and words to achieve greater harmony with those around me.

A Celebration of Love

"Within each of us, there is an insatiable desire to love, to be loved! The love we seek is much more than the euphoric butterflies-in-the-stomach feeling that a new romance brings: it is also the precious consolation of revealing my innermost self to someone else, of being accepted unconditionally and surrounded with good care. It is the deep feeling of tranquillity and peace of mind that comes from an intimate and close relationship with another human being."

— DAPHNE ROSE KINGMA

Today, I celebrate love. Valentine's Day hasn't always been a happy day for me. It used to be a day to take stock of my love life and the results weren't always what I would have wanted them to be. But now, I'm ready to open my heart and my life to love. Even if I may not be in the ideal situation right now, I can bring love to all my relationships. By opening my heart and my mind to love, I am opening my life to others. I seek to create a climate of mutual support, communication and tenderness with all those who want to get to know me and to share my life. Today, I open my life to love.

Organizing My Life

Today, I understand the importance of organizing my life. I use truth to identify all the possibilities available to me. I plan my life based on my own needs. I know that I can be happy by being what I really am, and I take pleasure in deciding what my future will be.

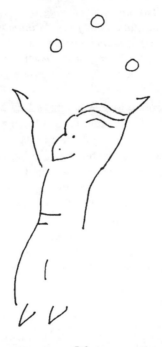

Good and Evil

"Let a benevolent person do good things with all the zeal that a malevolent person uses to do evil."
— SHALOM ROCKEACH

Fortunately, I have always been able to differentiate between good and evil. Deep inside me there is something that tells me what gesture to make or what path to follow. But when I let myself be influenced by others or by the excitement of the moment, I lose my way and I can't see clearly anymore. Today, I take the time to listen and to follow my inner voice. I choose the best solution based on my principles and my values.

Opening My Senses

Today, I listen to everything around me. I take the time to appreciate life and I have discovered that I am a sensual being. I see that life is very diverse: the sound of the wind in the trees, colors, shadows, textures, the sweet fragrance of flowers. Each of my senses is like an antenna. The more I look, the more I see how beautiful the world is. I give myself the right to discover the world and to appreciate it.

Facing Challenges

I reinforce my ability to face obstacles and problems. Over the years, I've learned that I have to face up to the situations and difficulties that life brings me. Sometimes I caused them myself and sometimes they seemed to come from a source that was beyond my control. However, I saw that by facing the obstacles head-on, I became stronger and less dependent on my environment and the situations in my life.

Change

"When we undergo change, our consciousness and our view of the world is transformed. We go from one reality to a different one, in full awareness. Through this type of change, we grow and transcend into a higher state of being, to higher, more powerful and more peaceful levels of our own being. At the same time as we experience greater personal power and the full potential of the choices we make, we also begin to shoulder our responsibilities so that our life can unfold as it should."

— CHARLES L. WHITFIELD

Today, I give myself all the tools and all the support I need to continue my transformation and to make it successful. Deep inside I felt that I had to move forward because I was no longer able to accept the truth or the lives others chose to live. I know that change is a process of questioning oneself but I am able to take on the challenge because it will bring me to new horizons, to happiness and to peace of mind.

Today, I accept change. I accept being the person I truly am. I will follow my own instinct and I will find the peace of mind I have always wanted.

Being My Own Advisor

"Believe nothing, oh monks, simply because it is said. Do not believe what your teacher tells you simply because of your respect for him. But if, after examination and analysis, you judge the principle to be sound, to hold the promise of goodness and well-being for all living beings, then believe in it and let it be your guide."

— BUDDHA

I have realized that each and every one of us has opinions. These opinions and viewpoints can be very interesting and can show us the truth. But I have also realized that I must go forward and discover things for myself. I have to live through my own experiences, examine facts myself, and lastly, I must draw my own conclusions. Our society of experts and specialists has made us less capable of looking for the truth ourselves. Instead, we tend to rely on the judgements, analyses and theories of others. But in the final analysis, I know that I must live according to my own principles, my own truths and my own values. To determine these truths, I must set out on a journey to find them wherever they may be. Today, I respect the opinions of others but I base my decisions, my values and my life on the truths that I have experienced and tested myself.

It's Warm Inside

The month of February is particularly harsh. During this month, summer seems very far away. You can see the hardship of winter on people's faces and daylight seems to be a rare pleasure. I see that there are people around me who find life hard and who have a difficult time handling everyday problems. Today, I make small gestures of tenderness and affection. I spread only good news and I offer words of encouragement to the people around me. Today, I am sunshine and light. I bring warmth to those who share my life.

Beyond Suffering

Today, I realize that I have gone beyond the need to suffer. I have realized that suffering has no value in itself. I used to associate suffering with change and spiritual growth. So when I was suffering, I used to tell myself that the situation was natural and that I had to suffer to grow and to reach a higher level of awareness and maturity. But suffering doesn't make me a nobler, more spiritual or more honest person. Suffering simply makes me a person who suffers.

There is a practical side to suffering, however. When I don't feel comfortable with who I am, when I suffer emotionally, there is a reason. Something in my life isn't as it should be. So in times of emotional turmoil, I identify the reason and I make the appropriate changes.

What I Resist, Persists

I accept the fact that I cannot run away from problems and difficult situations. Sooner or later, I have to face the music. The best decision is facing up to problems as soon as they occur.

What I run away from eventually catches up to me. What I refuse to face continues to dog my life. Such is the universe. So I have resolved to face things head-on with the intention of handling each situation as it presents itself. When I use this tactic, when I face things, inevitably I find the road to truth and happiness.

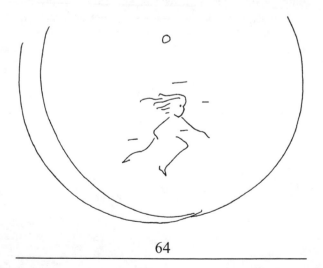

Life's Simplicity

"When we do tasks over and over again, we begin to recognize the natural cycles of growth and deterioration, of birth and death; thus, we realize the dynamic order of the universe. 'Simple' work is work that is in harmony with the universal order that we perceive in the natural environment."

— FRITJOF CAPRA

I spent a good part of my life reading the works of great scientists discussing the true nature of human beings, their hidden impulses, the hierarchy of their needs and the depth of their subconscious. But I look around me and I see that these theories have very little positive effect on the quality of life of individuals, on their health and on their spiritual fulfillment. I have decided to leave these complicated theories to others. Today, I live as I want to. I listen to my heart and I look for simplicity in my relationships with others. I keep away from loud and complicated people and I share my life with people who have common sense. I rejoice in the simple and beautiful things that life brings me every day: work I find enriching, faithful and sincere friends, good health and a clear mind.

The Truth of the Moment

"If I am unable to find pleasure in washing the dishes or if I want to get the job over with as quickly as I can so that I can sit back down at the table to eat my dessert, I am equally unable to enjoy my dessert! As I pick up my fork, I am thinking about the next task that awaits me and the dessert's texture and taste and all the pleasure it brings, fade into the background. I will always be dragged into the future and I will never be capable of enjoying the present."

— THICH NHAT HANTH

I have spent a good part of my life rushing forward, thinking that happiness, success and true love were just around the next corner. I told myself that someday, all the different aspects of my life would fall into place and then, finally, I would be able to start living. Now I no longer live this way. I see the small things in life as very important: small daily rituals, the color of the sky, the taste of good food and the happy times spent with sincere friends. These small pleasures fill my soul and keep me in touch with my inner self. Today, I say: "Why should I rush to reach retirement when real life is all around me every moment of every day?".

Detachment

"If we had a precise vision of everyday life, we could hear the grass growing or a squirrel's heart beating and we could die from the clamor that hides behind the silence. Things being what they are, the most agile among us advance under the weight of stupidity."
— GEORGE ELLIOT

I seek to cultivate detachment. For me, detachment is not indifference or an I-don't-care attitude. Detachment is the wonderful ability of the mind to observe events without being dragged into them. This type of observation is enlightened and increasingly part of my day-to-day life. I listen, I look, I observe, I try to see people as they are and to understand their behaviours and their lives. Detachment is calm, cool and crystal clear. Today, I cultivate detachment in my day-to-day life.

Master of My Destiny

"What we do today, at this precise moment, will have a cumulative effect on all of our tomorrows."
— ALEXANDRA STODDARD

There is absolutely nothing forcing an individual to live through any one experience. Without a doubt, I know that I am entirely free to choose my own fate. Only my decisions, my intentions, my perseverance and my tenacity will determine whether or not I reach my goals. I am the only person who can improve my fate. I am the only person who can predict my future. My decisions will determine what happens to me and how happy my life will be.

Today, I am in control of my destiny. I make my own choices and I shoulder my own responsibilities. I am a unique person with unique needs. I am the only person who can give me what I need.

What Can Be Transformed

Some people say we can change, we can transform our lives into something different. Other say that once you're an adult, your personality cannot change unless you live through a traumatizing experience. There is truth in both viewpoints. First of all, personality, identity, behaviour, values, attitudes, and the life choices an individual makes are essentially the result of learning, culture and temperament. All these things can change. But the fundamental being, the spiritual and true being does not change because, simply, it is. In very simple terms, change is the gradual or sudden discovery that the true being within us distances itself from what is not true and not essential.

Today, I rejoice in the person I truly am and I choose to let go of everything that is not truly me.

Responsibility

With time, I have come to understand that responsibility is not a burden or a test. Responsibility is my ability to accept, to receive and to have. I also see that as I accept full responsibility for myself, my actions and the things that occur in my life, I increase my self-confidence, my abilities and my control over my own life. When I accept the fact that I am at the root of all my life experiences, I become responsible and only then can I be in full control.

Sharing Responsibilities

Now I see that responsibility must be shared. In my friendships, in my relationships at work and in my relationships with family members, I understand the importance of sharing responsibility. When I take on too much responsibility and refuse to share any part of them, I am of no help to anyone. Conversely, when I let others shoulder all the responsibility, I do nothing to encourage team work and increase my self-esteem. Today, I try to see clearly and I work with others to strike the proper balance in my life.

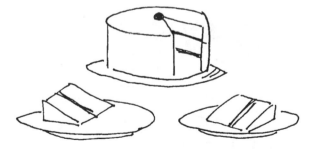

My Code of Ethics

I am aware of the importance of having a moral code. I have built my code on the truths that have always served me well. I have realized that if I really want to be happy, I must apply solid and consistent principles in my life. These rules of behaviour and these values are very simple, they guide my decisions and they help me live in harmony with myself and with others. To some extent, these rules are a moral code that guides me and helps me make the right choices. When I follow my moral code, I succeed inevitably.

Being Trustworthy

"I cherish my ideals and despite everything, I continue to believe that people are fundamentally good."
— ANNE FRANK

I keep my word and I keep my promises. Before giving my word or making a promise, I take time to consider whether this is really what I want to do and whether or not I can deliver the goods. Once I've thought things out, if I decide to give my word, I know that I will have to keep it. When I follow this guideline, I reinforce my self-esteem and I earn the admiration and respect of all my friends and all my colleagues. When I recognize the weight my word carries and how important it is, I am reliable and I inspire confidence. The people who work or live with me know that they can rely on me and I know that I can rely on myself in all circumstances. And when a problem or a conflict arises, I will know how to keep my word and I will know how to judge the situation fairly.

Foreseeing Consequences

I can foresee the consequences of irresponsibility. Yes,
at least for a certain amount of time, anybody can
laugh, have fun and ignore consequences. But eventually, everyone has to pay for their lack of concern for
the future. However, there are very sound and very
nurturing ways of experiencing pleasure without com-
promising body or soul.

Today, I foresee every consequence of my actions, and
in every situation I remember that integrity is one of
my fundamental qualities.

Growing

Life quickly becomes hell when a person decides to stop growing. Sometimes, people who are a little older tell me: "I can't change at my age." Once you take this decision, you begin to deteriorate physically, mentally and spiritually. Life is such that either we climb higher or we sink lower. No one can stay on the same step of the ladder for very long. Things may not always be easy, but if we give up, there will be no purpose to our lives.

I have decided to grow. For me, growing means that I am open to new experiences. I continue to learn and to progress. Growing also means that there are things left for me to do, I can continue to climb towards happiness, understanding, love and awareness. Today, I resolve to grow.

I Am the Architect

I know that I am the key player in my life and that by accepting all the situations and problems that I encounter as my own responsibility, I increase my control on my life and my fate. Being responsible doesn't mean taking on the burden of the incompetence or irresponsibility of others. However, I can do what it takes to surround myself with positive and helpful people. I can also agree to lend my support to others and to participate fully in their lives.

Responsibility is closely linked to action. When I agree to cause certain things to happen, I am taking action. When I refuse responsibility, I accept that other people and life's situations have an effect on me. Even when I feel that ultimately I am not responsible for a given situation, I know that I am the author of my feelings and my thoughts. Responsibility gives me the power to understand and to act.

Making Amends

"If I have harmed anyone in the past (regardless of how justifiable I may think my acts were), I must be disinterested as I admit my wrong and I must make amends and, whenever I can, reimburse material loss. The sooner I can do so sincerely and honestly, the sooner I will be free of the guilt that I have been carrying around unconsciously for all these years."

— ANONYMOUS

It is very hard to live in this world without making mistakes, without harming others, without abandoning our own principles. But when we set out to do good and when we are able to recognize our mistakes, we can mend our ways and adapt to life. Today, I agree to make amends whenever I make a mistake. I can examine my own conscience and I can own up to the harm I have caused. I am not perfect, but I am fair enough and conscious enough to restore harmony whenever I cause any harm to anyone.

Love Can Be Cruel

Society has given us an overly perfect image of love. We have been led to understand that love can make everything right and that if we love enough, we can overcome any obstacle. But love should not be blind. When we truly love, we should be able to do good things and at times, we should be able to set aside our feelings. When someone we love is causing harm to themselves or following a path that will inevitably lead to destruction, we must be able to love with firmness and detachment and we must be able to avoid falling into the trap of pity. Love is a combination of feelings of tenderness and affinity, but our relationships with our loved ones should also involve a sense of detachment and the resolve to show that we have the power of our convictions.

Today, I love with discernment and firmness. I no longer let myself be swept away in a flood of emotions that would only serve to make me a victim of love. I listen, I look, I seek truth and I refuse to abandon my commitments and my responsibilities.

The Power of My Decisions

I have realized that there is power in my decisions. I decide to act or not to act, to be or not to be. The world is driven by decisions. The fact that I can make a decision energizes me and boosts my self-esteem. With time, I have realized that I am the author of my own life. I am the person who decides. My decisions are extremely powerful. With the power of my decisions, I can change whatever I want to change, I can build whatever I want to build, I can destroy whatever I want to destroy.

At times I have underestimated the power of my decisions and after deciding something, I have let myself slide back into old behaviour pattern. Today, I decide and I realize that the situations I find myself in are the result of decisions I have taken in the past. When I want to make a change in my life, I look at past decisions and use them to make new ones.

I Am Responsible for My Destiny

I recognize that I am entirely responsible for my own fate. I know that external circumstances do not determine the road I travel. My intentions, my determination and my input determine my path in life. Today, I resolve to take action to control my fate. I want to open new doors, I want to find new possibilities and I want to broaden my horizons.

Congratulations to Me!

I congratulate myself for travelling on the road to self-improvement and personal growth. I deserve to succeed and to be appreciated because I am a good person. Not only do I congratulate myself on my accomplishments and the things I have done, I congratulate myself simply for being the person I am. I know that I can rely on myself. I am worthy of love and respect. Spiritual awakening, communication and providing an active presence requires a great deal of effort. And the reward for our efforts is an intense and full life.

Our Beautiful Little Planet

Today, I pay attention to all of humanity. I am aware that I am part of the human race and that I am partly responsible for the humans who live on this planet. Today, I use my imagination to see how I can contribute to improving living conditions on this planet.

I am responsible for my environment. When I see what we've done to this beautiful planet — pouring our pollution into its water and air, destroying wild animals and plants — I cannot be indifferent. I've been blinded by economic arguments to explain why forests are destroyed and why rivers are driven from their natural beds. All to maintain our precious lifestyle. All to benefit a very small number of people. From now on, I resolve to protect this planet's environment.

I Celebrate My True Self

Since I've decided to be myself, I realize that I am what is most important in my life. By making my own decisions and by choosing to see things exactly as they are, I let my true being shine through. And this experience brings me the joy and pleasure of accepting myself exactly as I am.

The more I discover about myself, the more I realize that I am wonderful. Each day, I discover something new about myself. By learning to meet my own needs, I also understand that I am a unique and very strong person. I can act positively and creatively. Today, I accept the feelings others inspire in me and I resolve to listen to those around me.

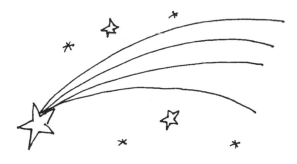

My Natural Kindness

Today, I let my natural kindness shine through. Kindness creates room for joy and freedom in my life and in the lives of others. When I am good and benevolent, I rise above the fight for survival and I reach a much nobler and more enriching level of action. Today, I am fully aware and awake, and I resolve to create a kinder and gentler world.

Kindness has nothing to do with the fear of not being loved; it stems from a generous heart and an open mind. I am not kind only because I want others to recognize my kindness. Instead, I seek to show my true colors in all aspects of my life.

The Power of a Smile

I have experimented with smiling at people who happen to cross my path. To my surprise, they all answer with a smile of their own. I've often wondered why people I don't know choose to react to a gesture as intimate as a smile. I think I've found the answer: human beings want to create ties with others and they leave their doors wide open to the opportunity of showing their openness.

A smile is an extremely powerful tool for communication. It shows your desire to communicate and it shows your good intentions. A sincere smile is an outstretched hand, a bridge that someone else can cross to reach you. Today, I recognize the power of a smile I smile to break through isolation and to create ties of friendship and compassion.

Learning to Love Yourself

"What does loving yourself really mean? ... It is a daily process you can use to come to know yourself, to be indulgent with yourself when you discover less than perfect things in yourself and lastly, to take steps to increase the self-esteem you need for your personal growth. Loving yourself means being able to admit to your weaknesses, it means knowing that even if things aren't always easy, you've always done the best you could. When we love ourselves and accept ourselves as we are, we are not afraid of growing, learning and changing."

— JUDY FORD

I will not wait on the love, respect and approval of others to love myself. Today, I give myself all the love and respect I deserve.

Where I Need to Be

I used to be very demanding of myself. I found it hard to accept my own mistakes. I was rarely satisfied with the results I achieved. I used to be very critical of myself. Ultimately, I wanted to grow and to achieve my goals, but I was much too demanding and critical of myself. And I was not entirely satisfied with myself. I didn't like certain aspects of my personality, certain aspects of my appearance. In a way, I was disappointed with myself and wanted to be different.

One fine day, all of that changed. I came to understand that I was who I was. From then on I was able to accept myself as I am and I accepted all the different facets of my personality. Today, I accept myself and I am generous and loving towards myself.

You are here

Asking for Forgiveness

"Denying responsibility when you've harmed someone can only reinforce your sense of guilt. The best way to find freedom is to admit to the error of your ways, to ask for forgiveness and to repair any damage caused."
— SHARON WEGSCHEIDER-CRUSE

I am a wonderful person and a human being. By making this statement, and by recognizing that I am undergoing a process of discovery and learning, I realize I can make mistakes. By taking responsibility for my mistakes and, if necessary, by asking forgiveness for the harm I have caused, I keep my road to self-fulfillment free of obstacles and free of guilt. Today, I see that I have the strength and conviction to recognize my mistakes and to ask for forgiveness.

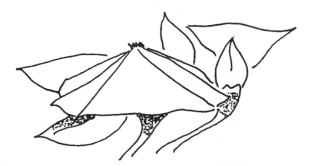

The Wounds Inflicted on Me

Today, I know that I can wipe the slate clean and forgive others for the wounds they have inflicted on me. When I decide to forgive, I free myself from the hold that revenge and hate have on me. I may not be able to forget, but I can let go of my anger and vengeance by remembering that the past cannot be changed. The only thing I can do is to use my experiences to guide me in my future relationships. After all, I am here to learn.

It is much too easy to let yourself be swept away by hate when someone harms you. But hate is a negative emotion that brings no good to anyone. So within myself, I choose to create a context of forgiveness, compassion and nobility. I know that the person who has hurt me has things to learn and life will be the perfect teacher.

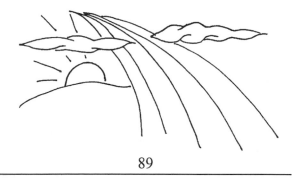

The Pleasures of the Soul

Today, I take the time to discover the simple pleasures of life. I call these day-to-day pleasures the pleasures of the soul because they are the activities that nurture my being and that within me spark a deep love for life. The pleasures of the soul include looking at a sunset, wearing a soft piece of clothing, enjoying a delicious meal. The pleasures of the soul are working in a garden filled with flowers and trees, building things with my own hands or listening to classical music. These simple pleasures bring me into contact with life itself and let me see the harmony in my relationship with others and with the universe as a whole.

My Intentions

Today, I recognize that my intentions hold the seeds to my future. Each intention is the beginning of a decision, the energy behind my desires and the power behind my actions. Today, I take a close look at my intentions because I have understood that they serve as the basis for what I experience and for what I make happen. If I set out with the intention to do good, to contribute to the well-being of others, life will bring me situations and experiences that are very different from those it will bring me if I decided that I do not want to be bothered with others. My intentions will determine my thoughts, my attitudes and my behaviour patterns.

Today, I adopt positive and creative intentions because I know that unconsciously, others can see what my intentions are. And my intentions are the root source of my experiences and my happiness.

Protecting Our Children

"As parents, we want to protect our children against all the suffering and injustices of life. This is impossible, of course. But what we can do is create an environment where children are physically, emotionally and spiritually secure. And we will succeed in protecting them all the better if we accept the fact that all the children of the world are our very own responsibility."
— JUDY FORD

All children need to know they are loved and protected. It's not easy being a child. Their small size and limited means make them dependent and vulnerable. We must all lend a hand in creating a safe environment for them. I accept my reponsibilities towards my own and other people's children.

The Secret of Prosperity

Today, I am successful from the material standpoint, but such was not always the case. Several years ago, I realized something very important, something that profoundly changed my work relationships: my prosperity is closely linked to the prosperity of those I serve. When I stopped worrying about my own prosperity and began working actively and intelligently to increase the financial wealth of others, my own income began to increase. The rule is easy to understand: when I offer a product or a service that truly contributes to the prosperity, well-being and happiness of others, I am rewarded. But I must be able to ask myself what the real motivation is. I must devote all of my energy to offering things that contribute truly to the growth and enrichment of others. Today, I am entirely committed to making others more prosperous and this is the source of my satisfaction and my success.

Looking in the Right Direction

More and more, I recognize the things that have a good influence on me. I have cleaned my life of faulty ideas and things from the past, things that hold me back and prevent me from being happy.

By dwelling on things that make my life better — love, joy, truth, satisfying my own needs and making my own decisions, shouldering my own responsibilities and nurturing healthy and lasting relationships — I bring out my true self and I express myself to the fullest. I deserve the best possible life and I resolve to take the means and actions to achieve that life.

Today, I recognize how important it is to dwell on what makes my life better. I resolve to rid my life of the things that destroy me and harm me. I resolve to open my heart to make room for love in my life. I resolve to focus my energy on things that are important to me and to my happiness.

People in Authority

In our society, we put people in power and then we spend four or five years holding them responsible for the worse possible behaviour. Elected officials can govern only if they have our support and our good will. In most cases they are people just like us, people who felt the need to make a greater contribution to society than the average citizen usually does. They cannot see into the future and they bring various degrees of talent to the tasks and responsibilities assigned to them. They cannot serve us without our approval, without our willingness to be served. Today, I take on the responsibility to support the people in authority in my city, my province, my country. I trust them and I try to give them the time and support they need to do what has to be done.

Asserting Myself

While I may be pleasant and polite in my dealings with others, I have also realized that it is important to assert myself. Asserting myself means showing others how to respect me. Asserting myself means calling attention to my point of view, my needs and my demands. If I don't assert myself, I can't be happy because I would be giving in to the needs and demands of others. I know what is best for me. I am an individual and I have my own needs and my own qualities.

When I assert myself, I should be as diplomatic as possible. If people feel insulted, they will not be willing to give me what I want from them. But if I defend my rights and if I repeat what my wishes are, without anger and without recrimination, I will get exactly what I want.

I Shape the World

"I am not a victim of the world I see around me. Above all else, what I see around me reflects what I am. I project the thoughts, feelings and attitudes that are important to me onto the world. So I can see the world differently by changing my eyes and deciding to see what I want to see."

— GERALD JAMPOLSKY

At times we all feel that we are victims of the circumstances in our lives, and not their cause. And indeed, I am not the only person in the world and I can feel the effects of the behavior of others. But I shouldn't feel that I am a victim of the world around me. I shape the world according to my perceptions, my attitudes and my behavior patterns. I am at the source of everything I experience. I create my own life. Therefore, I am responsible for the happiness each day brings me.

What is Not Me

"Stop shouting! Shouting at your children or your spouse creates tension and bad vibrations in your home and within your own head. Shouting is never a good idea. Nor is preaching, scolding, lecturing or pontificating. Stop repeating the same things and blaming people. Stop criticizing, directly or indirectly. Stop scolding, stop threatening, stop shouting, stop insulting. For some of us, this is easier said than done. We have grown up in families that shout and scream, where people lay blame, where they mock each other — where all of this seems like normal behaviour."

— JUDY FORD

It took a long time for me to realize that I can accomplish very little when I get mad, when I shout or when I use an aggressive approach. Aggression may bring me immediate relief because it lets me express my anger on the spot, but it always has a negative effect. Kindness, a willingness to listen and a sense of humour are all essential to good communication and effective exchange. Today, I know that when I show kindness and understanding, I win cooperation and support from others.

The Responsibility of Loving

Today, I see that love involves a major responsibility. When I love someone, I accept this person into the inner circle of my most intimate life. And I ask him or her to let me into their own intimate circle. I must respect, protect and support the people I love. I must respect their individuality and their needs and I must teach them to respect me. I must be open to learning how to love others. Love and friendship involve a great deal of responsibility toward myself and others. At times this responsibility can be hard to take, but it is the source of commitment and a sense of belonging.

The whole world changes when we bring someone into our own world through love or friendship. Through our closeness and our influence, we can help or harm someone, we can make them stronger or we can hurt them, we can set them free or we can dominate them.

Today, I understand that love involves responsibility and I seek to strengthen the ties of love and friendship by being aware and responsible.

Daily Opportunities

When things are chaotic,
I wish you inner silence.
When things look empty,
I wish you hope.

— ANONYMOUS

Each day brings with it the opportunity to contribute to the happiness and harmony others can enjoy. Each day is an opportunity to mend a quarrel, search out a forgotten friend, write a love letter, share some treasure.

Each day is an opportunity to keep a promise, forego a grudge, forgive an enemy. A chance to examine your demands on others, to think first of someone else, to appreciate, to be kind, to be gentle.

Today, I resolve to gladden someone's heart and share with them the beauty and the wonder of the earth.

Health and Well-Being

There is increasing recognition of the fact that health and well-being are directly linked to a person's emotions and attitudes. Some people even claim that there is a close relationship between our state of mind and our physical health. We know that we are responsible for our own health and our own well-being and when we fall victim to illness, life becomes terribly difficult. Therefore, each day I resolve to work at improving and keeping my health. By eating properly, getting enough sleep, relaxation and by exercising regularly, I can ward off sickness. When I recognize that I have to take care of myself, to love myself and to be vigilant, I am well on my way to good health and well-being.

Sobriety

Today, I resolve to live a sober and well-balanced life. I have experienced excess, inebriety and degradation. I have experienced loneliness, disappointment and lies. I have experienced poverty and hardship. Today, I choose to take full control of my life and I seek to use all the enlightenment and sobriety I can find within.

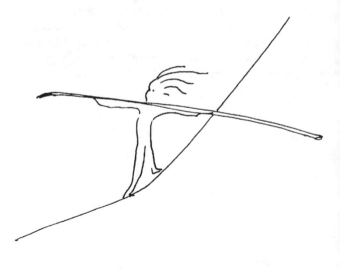

The Beauty Around Me

"I experience a great sense of tranquillity when I look through my window at the magnificent view to the north. I try to capture the precise moment when daylight fades into dusk and the sun is transformed into a magnificent spectrum of reds, purples and blues. One by one, as I overlook the scene, each street shimmers in the light, more precious with each passing minute as day passes into night."

— ADAIR LARA

Today, I awaken to the beauty around me and I choose to surround myself with beautiful things. I know that beautiful things are a source of pleasure and inspiration to me. I choose to focus only on the beautiful things in my world.

Maybe

Time has taught me that what can seem like a failure or a total loss may be something that in reality is very positive. What seems to be good or bad at first glance may be in reality completely different. Therefore I seek a degree of detachment and I look at things from different angles. Before forming an opinion or saying that something is good or bad, I wait and see how the situation will unfold.

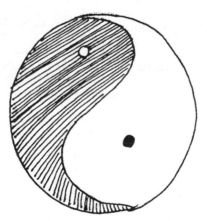

Now I Am Free

For a long time I was trapped inside myself. I think I had decided not to take any more risks and not to communicate with others. I kept certain things and certain people in my environment to convince myself that I was not alone. But with time, my life became very dull. So I decided to open my heart and soul to life and to others.

When I decided to be as open as I could to life, I was deeply afraid and apprehensive. But at the same time, I felt extremely energetic and powerful. Once again I felt the energy of renewal, freedom and adventure. Now I know that I cannot live in isolation, without the variety and the joy that freedom brings me. Today, I am free.

Spiritual Health

"In our search for material comfort, we look for and even glorify material well-being. Often, we have looked for material wealth to the detriment of our emotional and spiritual health, almost completely losing sight of the fact that spiritual health is the most precious asset we can possibly have. And because it is the most valuable of gifts, as we achieve better spiritual health, we have less need for material wealth. However, as strange as it may seem, once we achieve spiritual health, we are fully capable of filling all our material needs."

— ANONYMOUS

Today, I'll take time to think about my spiritual life. I know that I am someone who needs to cultivate inner resources. Spirituality is an important aspect of my life. I take the time to meditate on what I believe in. In my everyday life, material considerations often take up a great deal of time, to the detriment of my spiritual health. I recognize that my spiritual health is just as important as my mental or physical health and I nurture it. When I concentrate on my spiritual life, I feel light shining down on me and illuminating my path. I assert the fact that I am a spiritual being.

The Wealth of Maturity

"Today, I have a positive outlook on old age and the wealth it brings. Just as I used to cherish the wealth of the child within me, I value the things that growing old will bring me as I advance in age."

— ROKELLE LERNER

Even if my physical body grows old, I know that my heart stays young. I keep young by staying creative and active. So I take the phenomenon of physical aging with a grain of salt and I concentrate my attention and my energy on my true nature and on my true worth as a human being.

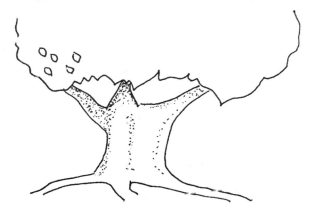

Laughter

I give myself permission to laugh. When things were going rather badly and when I was blue, I wondered how people could go on laughing. But laughter is extremely therapeutic because it lets the individual let go and look at things from a different angle. Today, I look for the funny side of life. When I make people around me laugh, I contribute to their happiness.

Confronting Indifference

"We realize that our achievements are but one drop in the ocean. But if that drop were not in the ocean, we would miss it."

— MOTHER TERESA

We live in a world filled with indifference. When we try to carry out a major project, we are confronted with the indifference of others. At times we can feel completely powerless in the face of so much indifference. But we must not let it influence or defeat us. If we keep our focus and persevere, we will reach our goal in the end.

Today, I realize that it is important to keep my dreams alive. I cannot let the indifference and sense of resignation I see in others discourage or defeat me. My good intentions and my resolve will support me as I complete each of my projects.

Saying Yes to Life

Life includes hard times and times that are rather sad. When you lose a friend or a close relative or when a relationship breaks down. When you realize that you won't reach one of the goals you've set for yourself. When you experience difficulties in your job or in your company. Life brings us a number of challenges and decisions that are hard to make. When you live through a deep disappointment, you may decide to give up hoping, to stop trying. But I believe that resignation is the worst possible enemy anyone can have.

Today, I choose to say yes to life. I recognize that there are trials and tests I must overcome but I will take them on with energy and optimism. I will not let life's circumstances defeat me.

The Joy of Reading

Today, I'll take time to read and increase my knowledge. I am here to learn and I know that others have explored and understood things that are still unfamiliar to me. So I make good use of the wisdom of others and I read to help myself grow. I also read for entertainment and simply for fun. The world of reading is the world enclosed in my imagination. When I read, I see various images that transport me to another world, to another reality.

Today, I embrace reading, I enjoy books and all the adventures, all the different faces, all the knowledge they contain — knowledge that nourishes and energizes my innermost being. I read attentively and judiciously because I know that there is positive and there is negative in the world of books. I will judge for myself and I will make the best possible use of anything that can help my personal growth and well-being.

Resting

"On some days, I realize that a great deal of things can shatter my life. At times like these I feel torn apart, I feel agitated and nervous. Now I know that this is a sign telling me that it is time to rest. When I am calm, I can look inside myself, I can relax, I can find new strength."

— EILEEN WHITE

I've always liked to sleep. Sleep is a way to relax totally and to find new mental and emotional energy. When I neglect to get enough sleep, I begin to be negative and I tend to see everything as very bleak. So now, when I feel impatient or angry, I know that I need a few more hours of sleep.

Today, I set aside enough time for relaxation and sleep because I know that life is much more beautiful and much easier when I am well rested.

Admiration

Admiration is the feeling of joy and fulfillment we experience in the face of something or someone we see as beautiful or noble. I have the possibility of developing the ability to admire myself and the people around me. I believe that I can even nurture admiration and use it in each of my relationships. Admiration is noble and it lifts me above the world of mockery, hatred and conflict.

Today, I nurture admiration in all of my relationships. I know that it is important to establish sound and lasting relationships. Admiration is one of the most important aspect of any relationship.

The Promise of Spring

Today, I am happy to see that spring is here at last. With spring comes the energy of rebirth and growth. Today, I celebrate spring, my own personal season of rebirth and growth. Now I can shed my old and worn coat and I can bathe in the spring light. I am ready to grow and to experience renewal. I use the energy of spring to find my own wings.

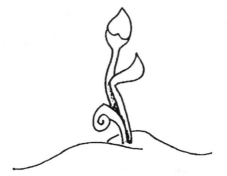

Freedom

"We live in an upside-down world. What we think is important is often completely trivial in reality. We work hard at building sand castles. We rush to fill our lives with conquests and possessions but we are blind to the only true goal: freedom."

— Marc Alain

Today, I embrace the freedom to explore, to take risks, to be spontaneous and to do what I need to do. Today, I am ready to give myself permission to embrace my freedom because I know that I am responsible. I know that I am able to live with the results and consequences of my new freedom. And I know that I will always be true and faithful to my inner self.

Making an Omelette

There's an old saying: you can't make an omelette without breaking eggs. Sometimes we have to be ready to do hard things to create something new. If we want to open a new company, we have to be prepared to leave a stable job and spend our savings. If we want to end an unhealthy relationship, we have to be ready to break ties, to say: "No, it's over." Today, I am not afraid to break a few eggs to get the positive results I want in my life. I know that I can make the right decisions and the right choices.

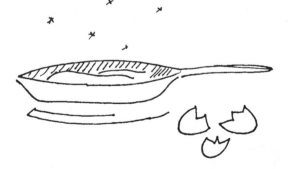

Finding Renewal

Today, I know that each minute is new, that each minute brings with it the chance for change and renewal. So I can shed my old coat, the coat I learned to wear as protection against the cold and my sense of being abandoned. They say that every cell in our bodies is capable of renewing itself. In the same way, I can renew myself as well. I can change attitudes, I can change my mind. I can use new glasses to see the world in a different way. I can discover a new truth that will change my way of thinking.

Today, I know that I can undergo renewal every minute. I rejoice in the fact that every single thing changes. Every single thing undergoes constant transformation. I will not resist the process of renewal and change. I will let the flow of renewal and change sweep me toward endless new possibilities.

The Need for Approval

"Today, I renounce the excessive need I have of winning the approval of others. In the dominating and dependent home I grew up in, my emotional security was based on the fact that I had to please my parents. So I learned to identify the least sign of disapproval on their part and I learned to let others control me. As a result, inside me there is still a small child who urges me to say and do things that will win the approval of those who are closest to me."

— ROKELLE LERNER

Today, I understand that I have no control over what other people think of me. Some people will like and respect me and others will want to exploit me and make me believe lies. I choose my friends wisely and I let others think whatever they want to think of me. Today, I know that I can live without the approval of others. I am free to think what I want to think and to do what I want to do.

Artisans of Joy

"Children are the artisans of joy. With their miniature bodies, they laugh and run and roll about, they bounce and take off in all directions. They get agitated when you take them into your arms, and they are so full of energy that that you spot them as soon as they enter a room. They like touching and tasting everything they come into contact with. And they can look into your eyes with an honesty that is so charming, that for a second you'll wonder how to respond. They do so many funny things... Life is full of ridiculous things and children have the gift of seeing them clearly."

— JUDY FORD

Children experience life creatively. They haven't learned to be cool and distant. They can enjoy every experience because they have no preconceived ideas. They truly see what is before their eyes. They approach life with a sense of constant wonderment. Today, I look at life through the eyes of my inner child. I have restored my ability to play and to touch things with my hands and to taste things on my tongue. Today, like all children, I experience life creatively.

Living One Day at a Time

The expression "Living one day at a time" was developed by Alcoholics Anonymous, a group that recognized that rehabilitation from alcoholism is something achieved one day at a time and one minute at a time. The individual who is trying to wean himself from alcohol must succeed in getting through one day; looking at a lifetime without alcohol is a thought that may be too threatening or frightening. A day without alcohol is a victory, one step closer to sobriety and control over a powerful dependence.

This fundamental philosophy of life can be useful when we try to put our life in order. It can help us through very difficult times by guiding us to small victories each day. It also encourages the individual to live in the present moment, and not in the past or the future.

I Am a Living Link

"We are living links in the force of life that moves about among us and plays within us, around us, uniting the furthest depths of the earth with the highest stars in the sky."

— ALAN CHADWICK

I am driven by a life force that inhabits me and that energizes my body. This life force is infinitely good and infinitely wise. I am this life force and it is me. I am a luminous and great being. In each of us is the very same tender and compassionate life force.

I place my trust in the life force within me. I know that my wisdom, my inspiration and my intuition come from the life force that inhabits me and binds me to all other beings in this universe. Every day, I turn to the life force within and I use its wisdom. And when the life force will leave my body, I will have no fear for I know that I will leave with it.

My Emotional Recovery

"At times we suppress or deny our feelings for fear that those who share our lives will fail to understand them or will refuse to accept them if we verbalize them. But it is only by honoring and recognizing my true feelings that I can achieve emotional recovery, move ahead and grow."

— SUE PATTON THOELE

My emotional recovery depends on my recognition of my own feelings and my emotional state. By admitting my feelings honestly, I can begin to settle my life and see my motivations and my actions more clearly. By admitting that I have been hurt and by crying over my pain, I take control of my anxieties and my frustrations. Today, I recognize that I am human, that my feelings are important and that they should be expressed.

Keeping Up Appearances

In our society, appearances are very important. Simply by keeping up my appearance, I can open a great many doors. People tend to look at me and to listen to me instead of focusing on my appearance. Of course, people like to create an effect through their appearance. But I am aware of the effect that I create with my clothing and my physical appearance.

The Joy of Solitude

"Despite all the affection we have for our loved ones, it sometimes happens that when they are absent, we feel an inexplicable peace."

— ANN SHAW

When I am alone, I can hear myself, I can find my own space and I can feel my inner peace. Now I look for moments of solitude that bring me a sense of calm and that put me in contact with my inner self. I do not avoid solitude, I embrace it as I would an old friend.

In the past, I never wanted to be alone because when I was, I had to confront the ghosts from my past. I may still experience difficulties, but I know that I can surmount them. If I am filled with feelings of anxiety or anger, I busy myself with something else, I meet with friends or I simply use the phone to get in touch with a helpful person.

My Way of Being

"The only thing you have to offer another human being, at all times, is your special way of being."

RAM DASS

I can't really give things to others. What the people around me want is me! They want to get to know me. They want to contribute to my life. What I can give others is myself, my way of being, may way of seeing things and my way of living. If I wanted to drive people away from me, I would give them material things instead of the gift of myself.

Nearing the End of a Project

I have realized that the cycle involved in finishing a project includes two crucial moments: at the outset, I need a great deal of energy to set things in motion and to help them take shape and when I near the end of the cycle, I must persevere and achieve my goal. When I know this, I don't give in to discouragement. I know that I have to devote all the energy and all the time needed at the outset to get the project off the ground. There are specific types of difficulties in the beginning. I know that I must be patient and that I must take the actions needed to make my project a reality. Later, as I approach the end, I sense that I must cross another difficult stage. In the final phase, I have to confront my final resistance. I resolve not to give in to discouragement during this phase. Today, I give myself access to everything I need to succeed. I arm myself with patience, vigilance and courage. I understand that there are specific difficulties along the way each time I seek to achieve my goals and I avoid feelings of discouragement.

Maintaining Healthy Relationships

Some individuals are sincerely committed to the process of development and growth. They want to learn and to do good. Some individuals try to take undue advantage of others. They can easily lead us into unhealthy situations because they have failed to develop a very high awareness of responsibility. We quickly discover who these people are. They look fine from the outside, but they have no deep commitments and therefore, they tend to abandon people and projects at random.

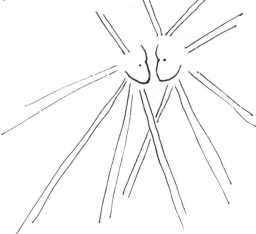

Gestures of Compassion

In our modern societies, there seems to be no room for compassion. We are wary of one another. We try to avoid contact and we don't want to get mixed up in other people's business. But if I open my eyes, I see a great many people who are suffering and working hard to improve their lives. I can be an instrument of love and compassion. Gestures of compassion can be simple and they have an astonishing power to heal.

My Greatness

We must ask ourselves a fundamental question: how far does my responsibility extend? I can readily admit that I am responsible for myself. I can also easily admit that I am responsible for my children and my immediate family. If I am a team leader, foreperson or supervisor, I am responsible for my sector and my employees. But beyond these immediate areas, I find it hard to define my level of responsibility. I have the impression that I cannot be responsible for areas that are beyond my direct control. But herein lies the crux of the question: as I extend my area of responsibility, I achieve a greater level of consciousness and fulfillment.

Taking the Time to Live

Feeling good implies that I take the time to live, to breathe, to have fun and to laugh. Each day is filled with opportunities to take the time to live. In our mad race, we often neglect to take the time to laugh, to have fun and to enjoy small moments of pleasure and relaxation. Today, I give myself permission to enjoy each moment and to have fun. Today, I feel good because I take the time to spoil myself and savor the things I enjoy. I pay attention to the small things that warm my heart and make me want to have fun.

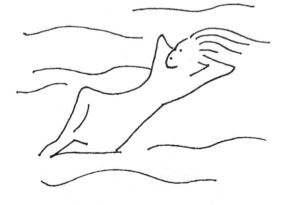

Work is Noble

"Generally speaking, security is only a superstition. It does not exist in Nature and most human beings never truly experience it. Over the long run, avoiding danger whenever you can is every bit as unhealthy as exposing yourself to danger whenever you can. Life is either a thrilling adventure, or nothing at all."
— HELEN KELLER

For individuals and society as a whole, work is the prime source of freedom and self-determination. When I work, I am useful and I shape a place for myself within society. When I work hard, I become indispensable. By being productive, I find self-fulfillment. To be truly free and happy, every individual must be self-reliant and self-sufficient. Working lets me lead exactly the kind of life I want for myself. By being productive and competent, I earn the respect and admiration of others. I can achieve all my objectives through honest work.

I Finish My Projects

"The first secret to efficiency consists in developing a deep aversion to any work that remains undone. Any work you set aside devours your energy and saps your efficiency. If you are passive when faced with undone work, you let an enemy crawl behind your lines and gain ground. In only a short while, your enemy will paralyze you completely."

— FRANÇOIS GARAGNON

The road to success and self-respect is paved with completed actions. When I leave something undone in my life, I feel the effects. I resolve to finish all of my projects. If from the very beginning, I get the feeling that I will not be able to complete a project, I just don't start it.

In the past, I didn't always finish all the projects I undertook. There was always a good reason for leaving them undone: too little time, too little money, not enough interest, etc. But now, I see that the road to success and self-respect is paved with cycles of completed action.

Standing on Your Own Two Feet

I like being able to stand on my own two feet. I always knew that if I wanted to be truly free and happy, I had to be self-reliant and self sufficient. At times I'm afraid that alone, I may not be able to meet all my needs. But now I know that no other person on earth can support me and love me as much as I support and love myself.

I always knew that by working I could protect my independence and my dignity. I don't wait for others to tell me what to do or what not to do. I am a competent and productive person. When I work, I achieve self-fulfillment.

Down with Procrastination!

I take action! Too often I've waited before taking on certain problems or certain difficult situations. My days of procrastination are behind me! No matter what I'm faced with, I take heart and I take action. I know that I am responsible enough and capable enough to handle the consequences of my choices and my actions.

Financial Independence

I am working to achieve my own independence. I see how our society encourages debts and dependence on financial institutions. Today, I am working on paying back my debts. I borrow only if I know that I am able to pay back my debt quickly and I use my financial resources intelligently so that I can enjoy financial independence.

Corruption

"Corruption can make people very rich. But those who use it as a means to get rich should know that one day, they will be unable to find themselves at peace anywhere under the sun."

— FRANÇOIS GARAGNON

Of course, I work to earn a living. But I will never jeopardize my personal principles for the sake of financial gain. I am intelligent enough to recognize that crime and corruption sometimes look harmless and unthreatening from the outside. The consequences of small dishonest gestures aren't always clear and easy to see. But even though it's easy to commit small crimes without ever getting caught, each of us has to live with ourselves day in and day out, for the rest of our lives. In the end, deep in our hearts we know that we have committed a crime or willingly harmed another person.

I Am My Own Company

I've learned to look at myself as if I were a company. A company has a mission, objectives, resources and a work force. I know that I must invest in my own professional development. I must define my mission and my objectives. I must acquire and maintain productive resources. I must seek to increase the efficiency of my work force. In many ways, I am the president of my own company and I must try to be a good administrator and an energetic entrepreneur.

Wealth

Now, I set my sights on wealth. Wealth is the quick and sustained increase in my productivity and my assets. I know that anything that has stopped growing eventually stops existing, so I resolve to increase my production and to make sure that my assets are growing. When I keep this goal in mind, I feel stronger and I feel more self-reliant.

I Reap What I Sow

"Anyone who is willing to work to achieve self-esteem has more than earned it and all the good things it brings with it as well."
— SHARON WEGSCHEIDER-CRUSE

I reap what I have sown with my labour and my perseverance. I congratulate myself on all the fine work I've done and I take pleasure in the fact that now I am the person I want to be. I find my satisfaction not so much in accomplishments that have a material aspect, but in my heart. Now I can trust myself and my feelings.

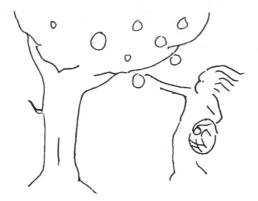

I Learn More and More

The key to my success lies in *learning more and more*. Curiosity is the source of invention and discovery. I know that I must do my own research and find my own answers. The more I learn, the more knowledge I can use to enhance my performance and the quality of my work, the more self-fulfillment I find. I realize that education is not simply the formal type of learning and teaching we find in schools. I must work at learning new things each day and every day, throughout my entire lifetime.

Today, I am open to learning as many new things as I can. I am here to learn and to grow. I know that by learning, by increasing the pool of knowledge I have, I am well on my way to self-fulfillment. I no longer look to experts and gurus for answers, I do my own research. The focus of my research is my own personal truth.

The Spiritual Side of Work

"Generally speaking, accomplishment implies a certain type of power, of control, of mastery, of commitment and of belief that a particular individual can accomplish a specific task. On a higher level, it does not mean simply accomplishing a task, but also being aware that the task has been accomplished. Indeed, at the highest level, accomplishment is probably the feeling that one has contributed to something, which in itself makes the task worthwhile."

— CHARLES L. WHITFIELD

Beyond any other consideration, work enables the individual to rise to the highest ranks in society. But work also has a spiritual side to it. By working, I recognize that I am the architect of my own life. I am aware that there is always something to do and something that I can contribute to. By working, I strengthen my relationship with myself and with others. Work is virtuous because it brings me self-love and freedom.

Interest

Most of us have heard the expression "The more you have the more you want". Instead, I say: "The more you like your work the more interest you have in it." The people who don't like their work aren't those who work extremely hard, but those who take it too easy. Bureaucracy and the division of labor have left us with jobs that are often repetitive and monotonous. But since individuals find their self-worth in their jobs, they must look for work that reflects their aspirations and enable them to find self-fulfillment.

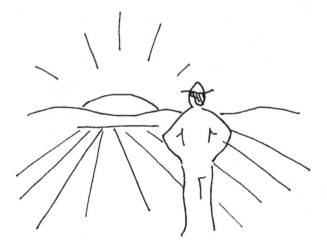

Being Punctual

Being punctual is one of the values I embrace in all aspects of my life. I know that being punctual is extremely important for people because they have often been faced with unpleasant surprises or worse, they have been rejected or abandoned. When I am punctual, I make those around me feel secure. When I am punctual, I am really saying: "You are important to me and so I am respecting the commitment I made to you." Elaborate explanations cannot replace the simple statement you make when you are punctual. Being punctual is one of life's virtues.

Action

Today, I take action and when I take action I feel a sense of fulfillment. I don't take action simply for the sake of action itself. Instead, I strive to create a desirable and lasting effect. I know that when I take action, not only do I have to make a decision, I have to carry it through and persevere until I have reached my objective.

Persistence

Today, I can enjoy the results of my persistence. The universe respects and embraces only those who show persistence. Persistent individuals who refuse to give in to appearances, mediocrity, dishonesty and cowardice will not be swallowed up in the torment that will emerge when the physical universe gives way and releases the truths it holds.

Life is an Adventure

"Today, I live life to the fullest: I jump head-on into the adventure that is life. I will not hide from risks. For too long my life has been marked by the boredom of routine. Looking for security, I let myself sink into a routine that eventually began to feel like a grave. Today, I want to explore and broaden my horizons on the physical, mental and spiritual levels. I want to feel the euphoria of new experiences."

— ROKELLE LERNER

I believe that I can create precisely the life I want to live. I do not have to compromise. I can be happy and fulfilled in all aspects of my life. When I treat life like a wonderful adventure, I am open to discovering new things and living new experiences. I can redesign my life with new and unknown elements. Today, I set out on my lifetime adventure with the conviction that I will find happiness.

Being Happy

"The real way to be happy is to love your work and to find joy in it."

— FRANÇOISE DE MOTTEVILLE

I have realized that work can be a game, that it can be a source of pleasure and joy. I don't wait for my work to be done for the day before I have fun. I have fun while I work. I don't believe that life begins when you retire. I can live and I can be happy while I am still working. When I work I build, I find fulfillment, I express myself. Today, I dedicate myself to my work and through my dedication, I find my inner self and I discover who I truly am.

My Talents

"If you grow what lies within you, what is within you will lead you to salvation. If you do not grow what lies within you, what fails to grow will destroy you."
— JESUS CHRIST

Each of us has talents of our own, qualities and aptitudes that are specific to us and that serve as the basis for our fulfillment. When we look for a job or when we want to begin a new career, we should ask: How can I use my specific talents in the course of a job that will bring me pleasure? There is a relationship between my aptitude, my talents and my strengths and the type of work that is best suited for me. Too often, people choose a job or a career using criteria that are not truly important: prestige, what my family expects of me, salary, location. I have qualities that are unique to me. I must accept the challenge of developing my abilities and my talents independently from any preconceived idea or any exterior factor. I must be loyal to my nature and to my talents. By choosing a job that is suited to my inner nature, my personality and my talents, I maximize my chances of succeeding. And even though I may not earn a very high salary, I will be happy and fulfilled.

Doing What is Necessary

"Put all your heart, your spirit, your mind and your soul into the smallest of your gestures. Such is the secret to success!"

— SWAMI SIVANADA

I am aware that ultimately, I must rely on my own judgment and I must do what I feel is necessary. I can listen to the advice of my friend, my family, experts in various field, but ultimately, I must live with the consequences of my acts. So I must find within myself the specific responses to the situations and problems facing me.

I must be able to find my way in society. I must develop my own formula, my own recipe. I can borrow elements from here and there, but I must create my own strategies.

Today, I am happy when others share their advice and opinions with me but I know that in the end, I must listen to my heart and do what I feel is necessary.

Simple Work

"When we carry out a task that has to be done time and time again, we recognize the natural cycle of growth and deterioration, of birth and death; thus, we realize the dynamic order of the universe. "Simple" work is work that is in harmony with the order that we perceive in the natural environment."

— FRITJOF CAPRA

I believe that there is something very nurturing in the simple work that we carry out each day. In such work, I find equilibrium. When I carry out a task like cleaning my home, ironing clothes or washing dishes, I feel as if I am putting my life in order. These small day-to-day tasks require very little intellectual effort. So I can carry them out while I think about my concerns or while I plan other activities. Day-to-day work is a form of meditation for me.

Today, I carry out simple tasks and as I do, I put order in my life, I move forward.

Solving Problems

To succeed, I must face the problems that occur in my life and I must solve them. If I try to avoid them, sooner or later they will reappear and I will be forced to work even harder to solve them because of my deeply buried resistance to facing them. But if I develop an attitude that lets me look upon problems in much the same way as I look upon a visit from an old friend, I will never feel powerless. A problem can be seen as an obstacle or a barrier, or it can be seen completely differently. It can also be seen as an interesting variation on a familiar game, something that adds interest and excitement to my life. I can look upon problems with a positive attitude because they help me go beyond my personal limitations, to travel further on life's path and to become even stronger.

Today, I accept the fact that the key to my success lies in my ability to solve problems. Instead of running away from my problems, I greet them with open arms.

Building a Future

"You can't get spoiled if you do your own ironing ."

— MERYL STREEP

Work brings me back to what is crucial in life: building. I am the only person who is responsible for my life and my well-being. When I work, I find fulfillment. I contribute to society. I am entirely responsible for the place I make for myself within my family, within my community and in the world. When I let others work for me, I lose that place. Today, I roll up my sleeves and I work gladly.

I can get up every morning to earn my living. That in itself is very honorable. But I am capable of doing more. With my work, my intelligence and my creativity, for myself, I can build a greater future, I can found a company and I can bring it to the point where it can survive when I am gone. I am here to create links, to go beyond my limitations, to bring something that the world didn't have before I came along. Today, my work lets me build something greater, something new, something beautiful that can contribute to the lives of the beings who share this planet with me.

Accepting Help from Others

I had decided that I wanted to work on my own. I would get things done myself. I didn't need help from anyone else. My decision was based on the idea that I would achieve the best results by working alone and that involving others would only slow me down. Obviously, I reasoned this way because of negative past experiences. And based on these experiences, I decided to shut the door on others. With time, I realized that I could work alone only for a certain amount of time. Eventually, I had to accept help from others.

Team work can be a magnificent experience. But I had to face the fact that team work is something completely different from individual work. Team work calls for a great deal of communication, good will and basic courtesy. Team work brings enormous rewards. Team members build together. Teams can accomplish great things. Each member of a team enjoys unbelievably beautiful experiences of sharing and complicity.

Forget Retirement

"The most persistent and urgent question in life is: What are you doing for others?"
— MARTIN LUTHER KING JR.

In society, there is a certain discourse that goes like this: *By working intelligently and saving, I will be able to retire when I am young enough to really enjoy life.* This form of thinking is not truly productive since it pushes us into the future and makes us forget the magic of the present moment. Work is not something we do while we wait for retirement. Work is real life, here and now. Today, I like my days to be filled with activity, meetings and commitments. For me, life — real life — is now. I would never trade the intense life I'm enjoying now for any other, even retirement!

The Courage to Succeed

It takes just as much energy to succeed as it does to fail. There is just as much work and just as much difficulty in success as there is in failure. I realize that I must work actively to grow or to stay small. The exact same effort is involved in both cases, but it is directed differently. When we put no effort or energy into achieving our goals, we spend enormous energy resisting what comes naturally. Human beings naturally strive to achieve and experience success in all of their undertakings. It takes a great deal of effort to stop short of accomplishment.

Therefore, success calls for a certain degree of courage — the courage to be aware of the decisions and obstacles that we put in our own path to success. This exercise requires enormous discernment and precision. But when we set out to take stock of our limitations, of our decisions and of our barriers, we have already opened our minds to success.

Success requires another form of courage — the courage to live a greater and more demanding life and to go beyond the personal limitations we have known so far. Today, I make positive use of my courage and I move forward to greet the future.

I Am Creative

The more I discover about myself, the more I realize that I have an astonishing ability to create. I also discover that I am responsible for this ability. I have the choice of creating happiness in my life.

As I grow, the ability to create is revealed in my aptitudes and my talents. When I express my creativity at work, in drawings, paintings, sculptures, writing or by any other means, I use my personal resources in a context of joy and love. The more I create the more I realize the infinite potential within me.

Today, I explore my creativity. I learn to express myself through my talents and aptitudes. My accomplishments are a source of pleasure and pride.

The Key to Success

"If you want to compress something, begin by letting it expand. He who begins by asking, asks for too much and in the end, succeeds in nothing."

— THE I CHING

There are not a thousand and one ways to succeed in one's professional life. First, choose a field you like and then work hard for a good number of years so that you fully understand all of the aspects it involves. By setting down solid roots in your chosen field and by taking your rightful place in it, you will earn the respect and cooperation of your peers. Changing directions and fields of interest often can lead to self-discovery, but it does not necessarily lead to success.

Today, I take the decision to continue working in my chosen field because I know that I will succeed in taking my rightful place within it.

The Power of My Dreams

"I do not know what fate has in store for you, but of one thing I am sure: the only individuals among you who will experience true happiness are those who will seek and find a way to serve others."
— ALBERT SCHWEITZER

I can formulate mentally the goals I want to achieve. If I want a certain result, I must be able to imagine it as if I had already achieved it. Such is the power of my dreams. I can imagine my future. In my mind, I can build a situation, a life context that I want to experience. My mental construct is a guide for me.

If I have no goals and no dreams, how can I realize that I am growing and changing? My imagination can guide my actions. Today, I use my dreams to guide me and to inspire me.

Other People's Labor

"A hundred times a day, I tell myself that my inner and outer life depends on the work of other men, living and dead, and that I must strive to give as much as I have received and will continue to receive."
— ALBERT EINSTEIN

I have realized that I must work every day to earn my place in society. I cannot be content with a life of dependence on the work of others. It may be very tempting to live at the State's expense, simply out of frustration or a sense of resignation. But I work not only because I want to earn my living. I work to strengthen my self-esteem, to come into contact with others, to contribute to the well-being of others. Today, I recognize the importance of doing my share.

What I Do is Important

"The smallest little task in day-to-day life contributes to the overall harmony of the universe."
— SAINT THERESA OF LISIEUX

Every task, every job that contributes to the overall harmony of the universe is good. Every trade has its value. The window-washer, the housewife, the plumber, the physicist — all play a role in creating harmony in social relationships. Today, I am proud of the work I do. I am happy to contribute to the harmony of the universe.

One Day at a Time

Just as you build a house by laying a foundation, we build our future with one action, one task at a time, and one day at a time. Today I have the opportunity of taking one more step towards my goal. I keep my goal in mind and I work hard at achieving it. I don't get discouraged because I know that satisfaction comes from a day filled with work well done. I take pleasure in doing my very best in all that I undertake and in this way, I increase my happiness and my sense of pride.

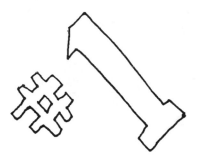

Communication

I am here to create links with other people, to communicate. Communication involves sending and receiving messages. Through communication, we can overcome loneliness, eliminate confusion, touch others and build our future.

Resolving Difficulties

I recognize that most difficulties and conflicts can be resolved through communication. When I speak openly and give others the permission to communicate openly, I am greater than my problems. Misunderstandings and quarrels cannot withstand the light of communication. The relationships I have with others deserve my frankness and my attention. I am honest with myself and with others. I resolve to speak openly at all times.

Doing the Groundwork

Before bringing up a difficult topic or sharing a criticism, I do my groundwork. I treasure my relationship with the other person, which means that before bringing up a difficult topic, I tell him or her how important our relationship is to me. Then I take the time to explain why I want to bring up this particular subject and I remember that I must accept the fact that I may be given a very direct answer. By doing the groundwork that good communication requires, I can achieve my goals and strengthen my relationships.

Reading Between the Lines

I pay attention to underlying messages. Not many people are skilled at the art of authentic communication. So they have to rely on more indirect forms of communication and at times, more deceitful forms. Of course, there are nonverbal messages. But there are also underlying messages that can go unnoticed if I am not attentive. So I pay close attention and I try to read between the lines. By asking the right questions, I am in a position to understand the other person and the situation more clearly.

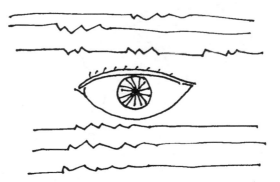

I Communicate with Myself

Today, I communicate with myself. I am in touch with my feelings and I am aware of what is important to me. Today, I am the most important person in my life. When I was younger, I was taught that it is not right to be selfish. But now, I know that it is healthy to give myself top priority in my own life. Today, I look out for Number 1. And Number 1 is me!

Listening with Your Heart

"Listening with your heart means being truly interested, open and attentive. It means wanting to listen, to learn and to be surprised — without the need to discuss, interrupt or advise (that's the hardest part!). Listening with your heart means not imposing your point of view, but discovering what life is from your child's perspective. It is listening with a sense of wonderment."

— JUDY FORD

Today, I listen with my heart. I know that if I really want a relationship, I must create a space that encourages communication. I can create that space by being receptive and open to others, to their needs and to the messages they communicate to me.

Freedom of Expression

I am very aware of the power of expressing myself freely. Freedom of expression is the very basis of growth, creativity and communication. I will use this privilege wisely to recognize and share the truth and to spread harmony and peace within my family and within my community.

Holding Out a Hand

"Today, I dare to take a new path where security and comfort are not the goals I'm after. I dare to hold out my hand to others and to be part of a society whose goals are peace, love, joy and healing."

— RUTH FISHEL

I say goodbye to loneliness and I communicate with others. If I am alone, the reason is that I have isolated myself and withdrawn into myself. If I am not alone but I still feel lonely, the reason is that I have stopped communicating with others. I can break out of my isolation and my loneliness by communicating. I can hold out my hand.

Adjusting My Communication

When I was younger, I had the bad habit of speaking curtly to other family members. With time and with life's experiences, I saw that my tone of voice and my natural intensity could be hard to deal with and could be hurtful to the people I loved and wanted good relationships with.

I understood that to communicate effectively, I had to make certain adjustments for certain audiences. Communication is something very personal. To reach someone, the communication must be adjusted to that person's "station". Some people are unable to hear kind and loving words. Others are unable to tolerate loud or strong-worded communication. So I look, I listen and I adjust my method of communication to make sure that I can reach the person I want to reach.

The Political Side of Communication

When I was very young I learned that I had to be careful of what I said, how I said it and who I said it to. I became so good at the art of self-censorship that I realized that I had stopped talking about the things that truly touch and affect me. But deep inside, I always knew that I wanted to be frank and to communicate genuinely. Now, I have a better understanding of how important communication is in my relationships and in my personal growth. I know that most difficulties can be resolved through direct and sincere communication.

Taking the Biggest Risk

Today, I take the risk of loving and being loved. I realize that I will not be able to grow and to learn if I base my life on accumulating material wealth and keeping my youthful looks. I need relationships and communication to live — they are as important and vital to me as the air I breathe.

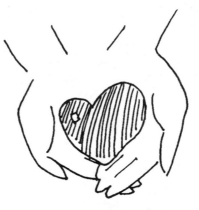

Verbal Pollution

Today, I promote verbal ecology. There are many types of pollution. The least known form is verbal pollution. Today, I think before I talk; I use words to establish links and not to fill in empty spaces.

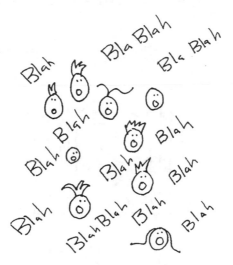

Speaking Openly

Now, I speak openly with my friends, my loved ones and my colleagues. With time, I have understood that the things that preoccupied me but that I was unable to share with others tended to take on a life of their own and to seem much more serious than they actually were. Now, when I am preoccupied by something, I talk it over with the right people — the people directly concerned.

Setting Out to Explore

Today, I am setting out to explore the world and I am expecting a wonderful adventure. I have come to understand that by staying alone at home or by settling into a strict routine, I miss out on the opportunity to live my life to its fullest and to achieve my full potential. I am beginning a voyage of discovery to find out who I truly am. By communicating, I now seek to build bridges between myself and others.

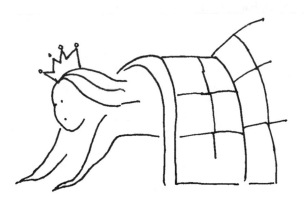

Smiling

When I smile, I open a door. My smile indicates to the other person that I am open to communication and that I want to establish a link between us. I can smile to invite others to communicate with me. I can smile to make people feel comfortable and to invite them to interact with me. I can smile to comfort someone. I can smile to say: *I love you.* I can smile to say: *I like you.*

A smile is a small gift. I can give it generously to those around me or simply to those whose paths I happen to cross in the course of a day. Today, I smile because I know that a smile is the prelude to positive communication.

My Need for a Relationship

How can I establish a relationship if I fail to communicate? Of course, some form of communication is nonverbal and communication can be part of silence as well. But a relationship calls for close attention and work. If I want to establish and deepen nurturing relationships with others, I must communicate.

Communication is not limited to saying words or to expressing opinions. Communication is a two-way street. I must be able to express myself freely and authentically and I must let the other person do likewise. If I refuse to send or receive communication, I can have no real relationships. I must be open to receiving and sharing communication to establish links and ties. Today, I want nurturing relationships in my life and so I choose to communicate effectively.

The Ties of Communication

I can establish or break the ties of communication. I must not be passive with regard to the phenomenon of communication. I choose to communicate or to be silent, and I choose to receive communication or not to receive it. I am responsible for the type of communication I have or do not have with others. This may seem a bit simplistic, but it is a fundamental truth: I am free to communicate or not to communicate.

At times, and for a number of different reasons, I do not want to receive a communication. This is my right. At others, I want to communicate. This is also my right. In the same way, I may not want to establish ties of communication with some people. If so, I am entirely free to break those ties. Today, I decide whether or not I want to establish ties of communication. And if I want to, I can break ties when the communication they bring me does not contribute to my well-being.

Listening

"It takes an ear of gold, an empty ear, to listen clearly."

— M.C. RICHARDS

For me, listening is a virtue. Listening means being attentive to others, being able to receive, hear and understand the message conveyed. Being open to communication is the basis of any form of cooperation or relationship. So today, I resolve to develop my listening skills. I am attentive to the communication I receive. I am receptive and I create avenues that others can use to communicate with me. In this way, I can break out of isolation and share my life.

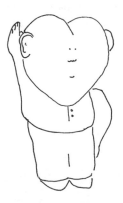

Self-Affirmation

It could be said that self-affirmation is the art of sending a communication directly and effectively, even when the other person does not want to receive it. It does not mean imposing a communication on someone else. Rather, it means getting across your point of view, your wants or your needs in a given situation. I cannot reach my objectives if I am incapable of self-affirmation.

Self-affirmation should never involve anger or aggression. This form of behavior serves only to break down the ties of communication. On the other hand, self-affirmation must be creative and patient.

Today, I embrace self-affirmation because I realize that it is absolutely essential to my self-fulfillment and my success.

Games

"When we play together, we feel happy and happy-go-lucky. We are freed from many an obligation and responsibility and we experience positively delicious times. When we have fun, the child within us awakens and we travel back in time, to a place where life was new and filled with possibilities. Because we are always young on the inside, we must have as much fun as we possibly can."

— DAPHNE ROSE KINGMA

Games are a very elaborate form of communication. When I agree to play a game, I agree to a system of rules, pre-established behaviour patterns and a very specific code of communication. My relationships with opponents and teammates are very, very different. In the game of life, if everyone is my opponent, my communication with those around me will be rather competitive or openly aggressive. If I see the people around me as my teammates, my goal will be to encourage communication.

Mutual Respect

Unquestionably, mutual respect is the most crucial element in communication. How can I encourage those around me to share honestly if I do not give them the respect and the right to express their own thoughts and points of view? How can I express myself freely if I am in contact with a person who does not respect me? Each person has a specific life experience, a specific vision of things and most importantly, the fundamental right to be themselves under all circumstances. Today, I encourage communication by showing my respect for others and by demanding their respect in return.

Showing My Love

The people around me, who love me, deserve my attention and my love. I recognize the people who support me and who let me express who I really am.

Today, I show my love for the people around me. I tell them how much I appreciate them and love them. I say thank-you for all that they've done for me, and more importantly, for all that they are, for the beauty of their true selves. I can show my love through gestures and through words. I choose to show my love unconditionally and unreservedly. I seek nothing in return for my gesture. Instead, I seek to increase my ability to love. I express my love based on my own feelings, not on the reactions of the people I love. I can express my love in many different ways. But I recognize that the most beautiful expression of my love is probably letting the other person be who he or she truly is.

The Unsaid

"It is absolutely useless to travel a road to preach; unless you preach on the road you travel."
— SAINT FRANCIS OF ASSISI

We all learn that an important part of communication is nonverbal. We communicate with bodily and facial expressions, with hand gestures, with looks, with sighs, etc. Actions also communicate important messages. Ultimately, we must rely more on actions than on words because words are easy to say, but harder to put into action.

I evaluate the people around me on the basis of their actions much more than on the basis of their words. Reliable and honest individuals keep their word and carry out their plans to the end. Less honest individuals can say a lot and all sorts of things, but they get very little done. I want to be an honest person who is worthy of trust and so I seek to carry out my projects as planned and to live up to my commitments. To protect my self-esteem, I apply my principles and I am true to my word.

Opinions

Everyone has opinions. Often, they are very interesting and can be very useful. They can tell you how to raise your children, how many types of flowers to grow in your garden, how politicians can heal our ailing economy or how you should live your own life. But there is an important difference between a person sharing a real-life experience and a person who is simply expressing an opinion. You can buy opinions on any street corner at a dime a dozen, but the advice of someone who has succeeded in a particular area is worth much more.

I am always interested in the opinions held by other people. Their opinions stimulate me and help me look at things from different angles. But I don't base my decisions on the opinions of others. Instead, I seek to increase my knowledge by carrying out my own analysis and experiencing things directly. And sometimes, I consult people with direct experience to ask for their advice.

Talking Isn't Necessarily Communicating

When you meet people who are compulsive talkers, you soon realize that they can't communicate. You may even want to shake them just to get the chance to get a word into the conversation now and then. Compulsive talkers can't really help us, they have their own very special path to travel. Maybe one day they'll run out of breath long enough to hear something else besides the sound of their own voices…

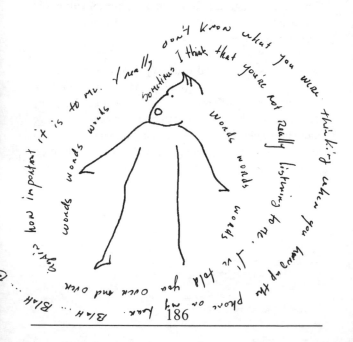

Communication and Health

There is a relationship between health and communication. Human beings naturally seek to create ties of communication and intimacy. But when, for whatever reason, human beings withdraw into themselves and stop communicating, they begin to lose their vitality and their health begins to deteriorate. Today, I seek to establish ties of communication with others and in this way, I work at maintaining my health.

The Beauty of Communication

Communication can be a source of joy and beauty. When I listen to background music, when I look at a work of art created with care and love, when I read a novel written with style, I am touched by the beauty of communication. Art is a form of communication. Whether a work of art is considered worthwhile depends on whether it communicates something and whether it is capable of echoing our perception of beauty.

I can also capitalize on the beauty of communication by using tender words and gestures. I can dress and decorate my home tastefully for the simple pleasure of communicating beauty. Today, I admire beauty in communications.

Two Hearts

"When two people are at one in their inmost hearts, they shatter even the strength of iron or of bronze. And when two people understand each other in their inmost heart, their words are sweet and strong, like the fragrance of orchids. "

— THE I CHING

Today, I'll choose to speak from the heart. I'll choose the words that really communicate and draw us closer. I'll take the time to really listen and understand. And when I speak, I'll show the other that I have understood and considered his or her point of view.

Communicating with the Supreme Being

I take great pleasure in saying my prayers before I go to sleep at night. I take this time to take stock of my day and sometimes, of my entire life. I pray to see things clearly. I pray to bring help to those I love. I pray to bring myself into contact with my innermost being and into contact with the divine universe. When I pray, I no longer feel alone. I feel that I belong to something and that I am worthy of experiencing life's good things. Prayer calms me and restores my hope.

Prayer is a system of communication. It enables us to establish very profound ties of communication with ourselves, with the divine within us and with the Supreme Being. I use prayer as a bridge between the earthly world and the world of luminous beings. Today, I pray for consolation, for better understanding, for greater calm and for greater serenity.

Genuine Communication

"Genuine communication, which we all look for, is the union of minds. Through the values we share, we come to know what the people we love think, what they feel and the way they may behave in a given situation. Genuine communication is a "connection" at a level where individual boundaries begin to blur and deep in our hearts, we know that we are communicating with the very essence of another individual."

— DAPHNE ROSE KINGMA

Today, I realize that when I communicate, I come into contact with another being. I am sensitive to this fact and I adjust my communication to reflect the nature and characteristics of that other being. I now that my communication will be effective if I truly want to establish a link with the other person's essence. So I take the time I need and I make the efforts required to enter into genuine communication.

The Power of Love

"One day, when we've tamed the wind, the oceans, the tides and gravity, we should explore the energy of love. Then, for the second time in the history of the world, Man will have discovered fire."
— TEILHARD DE CHARDIN

Love is not a feeling as such, although we may feel tenderness and an affinity towards another person. Love is something else. Love stems from our own will to love, from a fundamental choice that defines our relationship with human beings and with life. Love is the frame of mind that results from making the conscious choice to love. I choose love. I choose to be a loving person. And by choosing love, I transform my life, I transform the way I see the world, I transform my every action.

I Express My Needs

To be successful, a relationship must allow each person to express themselves and to fulfill their needs. A relationship cannot survive if it is based on suppressing the needs of one of the partners. My responsibility is expressing my needs and allowing the other person to find self-fulfillment within our relationship.

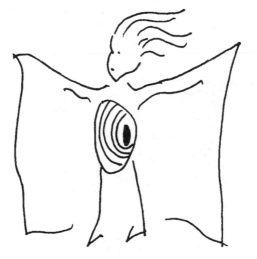

Letting Others Contribute

I realize that there has to be an equilibrium in the exchange that takes place within a relationship. When one of the two partners contributes more than the other, it is hard for the relationship to survive. In addition to giving, I must be prepared to receive. I am very vigilant when it comes to the exchange that takes place within my relationships because imbalance inevitably leads to disappointment and to failure. I cannot buy the other person's respect or love. Instead, I must insist on a balance in the exchange that takes place in each of my many relationships.

Insisting on Respect

Respect is an essential ingredient in friendship and love alike. Of course, I must respect the choices, personality and aspirations of people who share my life. But I must also insist on their respect. Many people are so preoccupied with the need for love and approval that they are afraid of self-affirmation. I can be loved and respected. I can show people how to respect me. I have come to the conclusion that a person who does not respect me does not deserve to be in a relationship with me.

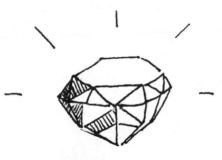

I am a precious diamond.
I deserve respect!

Romance

Romance is the champagne of life. It is the magic that has you want to dance the tango, gives you wings and makes you happy to simply be alive. Romance is surely an antidote to boredom. As soon as you let romance filter into your relationship, you are instantly elevated to a delightful state of well-being. Simply because of romance you feel beautiful and full of hope.

Today, I resolve to bring romance into my relationship with my significant other. I look for opportunities to express the depth of my tenderness and love. These wonderful moments of closeness and intimacy will reinforce our relationship and keep our passion burning bright.

Emotional Support

"No one can live his life solely for himself. Thousands of strings tie us to our brothers; intertwined in these strings, such as feelings of compassion, our actions are transmuted into causes and return to us as effects."
— HERMAN MELVILLE

I can accept the help and emotional support of others. It may be true that negative experiences have led me to believe that help and emotional support are signs of weakness and inevitably lead to betrayal and exploitation. In reality though, there are individuals who are worthy of my trust and whose support I am willing to accept. I am open to the help offered to me by others, just as I am open to offering others my help and my emotional support.

Loyalty

I give my loyalty judiciously. Loyalty is the ability to support and share responsibility with a friend, an associate, a spouse or a group. It is a very noble quality. When you show your loyalty you are saying: "No matter what happens, I will be by your side to bring you my help and my support." I want to be a person others can rely on, even in difficult situations. When I give my allegiance to someone, I never take it back. But like respect, loyalty must be earned. I am vigilant and I do not give my loyalty unquestioningly or blindly. First, I make sure that the person in question deserves it. Usually, I know whether a person or a group deserves my loyalty after observing them over a period of time and after sharing experiences with them. I remember that I have the choice and the right to give my loyalty to the individuals and the groups of my choice.

Identifying My Allies

I have learned to identify my allies. I analyze the behaviour and attitudes of the people around me and I choose to be around those who truly contribute to my well-being. I have also understood that I must stay away from those who slow me down and bring chaos into my life. I will not be intimidated. I am a free and responsible individual.

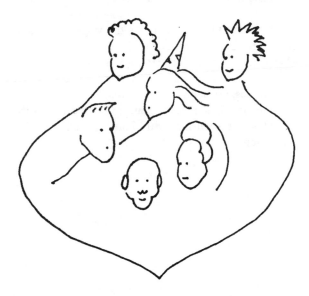

Marriage

I realize that marriage is a lifetime commitment, but not at any price. I thought that destiny had mapped out the entire road for me in this regard. I thought that once I had met the right person, all I had to do was sit back and let things happen. But life has taught me a different lesson. Marriage is something a couple creates together every single day. Each partner has specific responsibilities to shoulder and specific work to do.

An important factor determines the value and quality of a marriage: honesty. A marriage is doomed to fail when one of the two partners (or both) holds back certain things or is unwilling to share secrets openly. Secrets, lies, infidelities have no place in a loving relationship. It's as simple as that. Today, decide to live your love relationship with honesty and complete authenticity.

Faithfulness

Today, I clearly see the importance and the value of being faithful in my love relationship. A loving and committed relationship between two individuals is an agreement that can involve no holding back and no secrets. If I break the agreement, I destroy my own integrity and I doom my relationship to failure. Today, I believe in faithfulness because I have experienced the disastrous effects of secrets and infidelity. Faithfulness brings stability and harmony to a relationship. Infidelity profoundly destabilizes the relationship between a couple.

We often hear that the two partners in a couple can agree to or even encourage the other's infidelity. More and more often we hear statements like: "If we both have no objections to so-called infidelity, it can be healthy and normal". But the truth is that without a framework for moral behavior, the couple cannot last. Commitment requires constant work, constant vigilance and constant honesty.

Tenderness

"I can ask for affection without involving anything sexual. My need for love and human warmth is not linked to my sexual desire. I do not need to have sex with someone for that person to be my friend. I have the right to be hugged and caressed without paying with my body."

— ROKELLE LERNER

Today, I recognize that tenderness and affection are important to me. I can be open and I can ask for affection without encouraging sexual desire. I can want to be hugged without that want being linked to sexuality per se. I give myself permission to express my tenderness and my affection for my friends and the members of my family. I see how important tenderness is in my everyday relationships. I give and receive tenderness freely in my life.

The Gift of Friendship

I rejoice in the friendships I have created along life's path. I salute myself for making the right choices when I looked for friends and I forgive myself for giving up my trust and my self-esteem to certain individuals who were unable to appreciate the gift of friendship. Now I am capable of sharing my friendship wisely.

Opening the Door

Today, I prepare my heart to give and to receive love. I have always found it easier to love than to let others love me. I thought that this way, I could stay in control of the situation. But now, I see that this approach does not work. Today, I open the door to others.

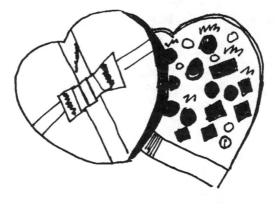

A Loved One

Today, I will contact a loved one I haven't spoken to or seen in a long time. Time and events have caused me to lose track of certain individuals who are dear to me. Today, I will pick up the phone and contact someone I miss a lot.

Touch

"... we recognize touch as a basic human need. Children who are deprived of another human being's touch do not grow properly and develop poorly even if they are well nourished and well protected. Touch is powerful during "skin to skin" contact... It seems that to feel "connected" and cared for, we have a great need to be hugged and caressed."

— CHARLES L. WITFIELD

Touch can be comforting. Touch can be reassuring. Touch can be a sign of tenderness and affection. Touch can break through isolation. A hand on a shoulder can serve as a source of encouragement and consolation. Holding the hand of someone you love brings you closer to them. I see the importance of touch in my everyday life. I am sensitive and I use touch to comfort and to bring others closer to me. I know that many people are less receptive to touch, so I am careful not to annoy them or make them feel uncomfortable.

Loving Yourself

"Loving yourself implies being able to admit your weaknesses, knowing that even though things haven't always been easy, you've always done as best you could. When you love yourself and you accept yourself as you are, you're never afraid to grow, to learn and to change."

— JUDY FORD

Today, I let myself love... myself! By giving myself this opportunity, I can accept myself for all that I truly am. I let my self-love grow and spread to others. I cultivate my love for myself and for others.

The Seniors in My Life

Today, I pay tribute to the seniors in my life: parents, grandparents, uncles and aunts. These people have worked very hard to make sure that we'd have a place in the sun. They have shown us so much support and so much love, they deserve a very special place in our hearts and our lives.

Modern society has completed changed the natural order of things. In this era of youth and speed, we have been encouraged to set aside the traditional family unit. In many cases, we have abandoned our seniors for the sake of a lifestyle based on more materialistic values. But now we see that these choices have had disastrous consequences on the family and on society as a whole. Many of our seniors live in isolation and in poverty. And our families are less strongly united and less close.

The Domination of Love

We see how, using love as a pretext, individuals seek to control and dominate. There are many examples of the forms this domination can take: a husband trying to dominate his wife; a wife trying to control her husband; parents who want to keep their children under their thumbs; parents who become emotional hostages to their children's blackmail, etc. Of course, this is not love, but something darker and selfish. Love is used as an alibi to hide our weaknesses and our emotional dependence.

This type of relationship is very confusing for human beings because they hear "I love you" while at the same time enduring painful experiences. They may come to believe that love is cruel, controlling and hard. But true love is based on freedom, respect and the sincere will to contribute. I refuse to be controlled or dominated in the name of love. I refuse to give in to the blackmail that love may be withdrawn. Today, I offer my love unconditionally and I avoid relationships that harm me in the name of love.

Two Souls

I have realized that a relationship is a contract. It is the union of two complete and independent individuals. We must define the parameters of our relationship, the conditions for satisfaction, the rules of the game. Together, we must create a common ground that is larger than our individual ground. If I change, that change will affect my relationship and will have an impact on the other person's life. If the other person changes, my life will be affected by that change because our lives are intertwined. I must respect my partner's growth and individuality and I ask that my individuality and my rights be respected as well. Today, I agree to grow along with someone else. I choose to share my life with the knowledge that my actions have an impact on our lives. I agree to let my partner grow and change within our relationship.

Rare and Precious Individuals

I am lucky to have met individuals who, through their love for me, changed my entire life. These people are more than friends to me, they are brothers and sisters. We recognized each other, we found each other. And despite the distance that may separate us, we are always close. Even though we may not see each other for a certain period of time, our affection and sense of belonging is always as strong. I have found only a few such brothers and sisters. I will keep them close to my heart throughout my life's voyage because they remind me of who I really am and how generous and rich life is. Today, I thank heaven for these rare and precious individuals who crossed the ocean of time to come to me here.

I am always a little surprised when, from time to time, I meet someone I instantly get along with, someone I feel I have known for a whole lifetime.

The Great Reality of Love

The problem lies in the fact that we use the word love to describe a wide variety of experience such as romantic love, affection, family commitment, etc. And true, they are indeed all manifestations of love. But love is a much greater reality — one approaching divinity. When I choose to give my love wholly and entirely, I put myself in the hands of a power that is much greater than I. Love's power, its strength is the profound manifestation and very essence of spirituality. Fundamentally, I am love. Therefore, when I choose love, I am in harmony with my true being and I find the serenity within me.

Letting Others Love Me

"By asking for what you need, you reveal your fragility as a human being and you invite the person you love to share his fragility The reaction to an expressed desire not only brings to the person who needs help the pleasure of seeing a need filled, it also brings to the person who fills the need a feeling of effectiveness as a person and a sense of being capable of giving happiness to someone else. In such moments, each of you have the opportunity of sharing your love and your humanity."

— DAPHNE ROSE KINGMA

Vulnerability hasn't always been viewed as a desirable quality. We know that when we are vulnerable, we may be hurt. So many of us have learned not to be vulnerable. There is another side to vulnerability: the ability to ask for help and love and the potential to receive both. In this sense, vulnerability is an openness and a receptiveness.

Today, I prepare my heart to give and to receive love. Today, I open the door to others.

How Can You Heal a Broken Heart?

Very few people have never experienced at least one breakup in a love relationship. These painful events have a lasting effect on us. We can cling to the pain for months and at times, for years. And when, at last, our heart begins to unclench, we love timidly, for fear of reviving the deep hurt. We realize that a breakup is a lot like the sorrow caused by the death of a close relative or a spouse. A breakup awakens in us feelings of failure, abandon, loss, anger and denial that can be very overwhelming. The pain runs even deeper when we have been rejected by a partner. Loss of self-esteem can lead to emotions and feelings that are even more devastating. But a broken heart can be healed through a new relationship, a resumption of the old relationship, time, therapy, crying, or tranquilizers. All of these remedies have no truly beneficial effect, although they may relieve the pain and fill a void for a certain time. The only cure for a broken heart is to grow, to change, to look straight ahead and to move forward with resolve. We must set aside the illusions we have when it comes to love relationships and we must accept the fact that everything changes and we are responsible for our own happiness.

Take Out Your Handkerchief!

Like waves on a beach, feelings come, and then they go. I do not cling to one feeling in particular; instead, I let come and then let go. Sometimes I feel sad, melancholic or angry. These feelings emerge suddenly and I let them come and then go without any great concern. And when they go, calmness returns. I have learned not to resist feelings. I embrace them. I welcome them.

Sexuality

Sexuality leads to tremendous confusion and difficulty in human beings. The spiritual being has no sexuality of its own; it can only experience sexuality from an outside source. But the body is driven by needs and urges that the human being must understand and accept. Some behavior patterns and perceptions contribute to the growth and development of the individual and others contribute to degeneration and confusion. When we listen to ourselves, we can act wisely.

Today, I know that sexuality belongs within a couple. I can experience a healthy and nurturing sexuality within a loving and committed relationship. Outside the context of a couple, sex becomes a form of slavery. I refuse to accept that it is normal and acceptable to view pornography and sexual degradation on just about every street corner. When I attach too much importance to sex and sexual relations, I stop my own personal development.

Loving Your Child

Showing we love our children is important. We can feel love in our hearts but we must also express our love and allow our children to express their love for us. In this busy world we live in, it is easy to let the days and weeks flow through our fingers and forget to say and to show, *I love you.*

Today, I express my love for my children. I love them, I tell them that I love them and I show it. Children are full-fledged human beings and they have a right to recognition and support.

Family Love

I have come to understand that the family is a place of sharing. The members of a family share beliefs, traditions, a lifestyle, dreams and ties of affection. But the family is founded on a type of contract, an agreement that enables it to protect its unity and closeness. The family can last as long as its members recreate this form of union from day to day. There is nothing inherent in blood or in genes that predisposes a family to stay together. Its members must have the firm conviction that the institution deserves to survive and grow.

I have learned that when the family is a zone of conflict, disharmony and violence, you must distance yourself for you own good and the good of the other members of the cell. This decision is always hard since we place enormous hope in the family and naturally, we want to belong to a unit that shares our ideals and our dreams. But no one individual can handle all that ails a family in disarray. Today, I surround myself with loving people who create a sense of security in others and who share my values.

The Quality of My Relationships

I have realized that to a great extent, the quality of my life is determined by the quality of my relationships. I can evaluate the quality of my relationships by the level of communication, the degree of exchange on both sides, the respect and affection I find in them. I must ensure that the people who share my life are honest and that they sincerely want to contribute to my well-being. This is crucial. When I see that an emotional or professional relationship does not contribute to my well-being, I must act quickly to reshape it or to end it.

Long-Term Relationships

Today, I cultivate and strengthen my long-term relationships. I take a few minutes to write letters or to telephone dear friends who still have an important place in my life. I know that the most important relationships are those that have withstood the test of time. These loved ones have accompanied me on my path through life and they deserve my effort to stay in contact with them. They will be thrilled to see that I think of them and our communication will serve to revive our deep affection for each other. Today, I celebrate the long-term relationships that remind me of who I really am and where I come from.

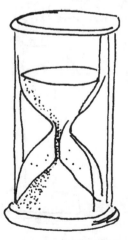

Sowing the Seeds of Love

Today, I sow the seeds of love in my garden. I cultivate tender relationships based on affection, communication and mutual help. Today, I accomplish the work my heart wants me to do.

True Love

"True love is much more than a feeling, a sensation, much more than a magical interlude of emotional inebriation that overwhelms us when the full moon is only a tiny sliver. Love is a range of behaviors, attitudes, and abilities whose practice creates and maintains a state that we call love. It is a dimension in the form of a relationship that satisfies, vivifies and heals, but it is also the product of a complex effort. In truth, love is "the work of love" that is apparent only when we realize that in addition to being a gift, it is quite an undertaking."

— DAPHNE ROSE KINGMA

Today, I agree to accomplish "the work of love". I see that true love results from a deep commitment that is nurtured each day by the decision to love a little longer, to love a little better.

A Revolution of Kindness

"My religion is simple.
My religion is goodness and benevolence."
— THE DALAI LAMA

I intend to start a revolution, a revolution of goodness and kindness in this society and in this world. I look around me and I see that a violent and perverse minority has managed to take a much too important place in our lives. I see that the kind and silent majority is sinking further and further into the quagmire of fear and acquiescence. I want to take back the streets, to take back the night. I want to live in a climate of security and respect. I know that we cannot fight against violence and perversion by using violence or by creating a police state. I believe that we can conquer all by working together to sow the seeds of mutual help, generosity and kindness.

A Tribute to Kindness

"Man should not consider his material possessions as belonging to him, but rather as belonging to all of us, so that he can share them, without hesitation, when others are in need."

— SAINT THOMAS AQUINAS

Now I let my kindness and my goodness shine through. Kindness creates places of joy and freedom in my life and in the lives of others. By being kind, I rise above the fight for survival or material success and I live consciously and responsibility with the goal of creating a better world.

Being Generous in Actions and in Words

"Kindness is a language that the mute can speak and the deaf can hear."

— C.N. BOVEE

I can be generous in actions and in words. In a world that is too often cold, rude and austere, my kindness can shine like a soft light from the heart, to illuminate the path of others. I recognize that my nature is fundamentally good and that by being generous, by opening the door to goodness, to love and to forgiveness, I am accomplishing my divine mission. My goodness and my generosity are expressed through listening, tolerance, patience, sincere help and respect for others. I let my profound nature guide me in actions and in words. I am filled with joy and I have no regrets.

Imposing Our Wishes

In the past, I had the habit of wanting those close to me to comply with my wishes. The result: countless failures! Others experience their own reality in life, they have their own education and they make their own decisions. Today, I observe and I listen before imposing my wishes and I say: Vive la différence!

Exploitation

Today, I cooperate with and reward the people who help me in my work. I believe that exploitation, control and domination should be wiped from this planet. We are at the dawn of a new era of mutual help and sharing. Those who believe that we can get rich at the expense of others are in for a very unpleasant surprise.

The Divinity Within

Today, I feel the divinity within me and I realize that I am complete and whole. I am not a tiny particle of God or an abstract and faraway force. I am an independent being, complete and divine. I seek to express my true nature through love, generosity and kindness.

Being Kind to Myself!

"Until you can accept yourself, you block the way that leads to the growth you aspire to reach. This growth comes from your heart. Be kind to yourself!"
— EMMANUEL

I understand that I must be kind to myself. I am my own best friend and I must be loving towards myself each day. If I take care of myself and if I am generous towards myself, I am more likely to be loving and good to others. Self-esteem is a precious asset. It is the foundation of all that I do in life. So I give myself all the importance and all the attention I need. This way, I can accomplish the greatest of things.

Listening to Our Children

"Talk to your children and listen to them, no matter what they say. Let them know that you're interested and that they have all your attention. Listening to them doesn't mean that you agree with them, it simply means that you agree to hear them out."
— JANET WOITITZ

It isn't easy being a child. The child comes into this world and must accept the conditions that prevail in it. He wants to be loved, accepted and supported. Because I was once a child, I know how often and how deeply I needed to be comforted and made to feel safe. I was very lucky because I was always made to feel wanted and loved. Today, I love children and I strive to understand and help them. I accept the responsibility of protecting children, of being a reassuring and helpful presence in their lives.

Generosity

I see very clearly the value of my generosity in a world that is too often cold, rude and austere. Generosity is a soft light that shines from the heart to light the path of others. Today, I know that I have nothing to lose by being generous. There are only winners in the game of generosity — never any losers.

Natural Goodness

Now I let others see my natural kindness. Kindness creates places of joy and freedom in our lives. By being kind, I rise above the fight for survival or for material success. I live consciously to create a world that is a kind and good place to live in.

Kindness has nothing to go with the fear of not being loved; it stems from a generous heart. I do not show others that I am kind just to impress them. I know that I was born kind.

Goodness, love and generosity are the instruments I use to improve my fundamental being. These small work tools exist only because of the suffering and the many problems facing us in this world. In truth, goodness, love and generosity are qualities that spring from my fundamental kindness. I need only listen to myself to hear the voice of kindness.

Forgiveness

"By forgiving, we gently refuse to fight against love. Forgiving is showing the will to see each person, including myself, either as a source of love or as someone who is in need of love."

— GERALD JAMPLOSKY

I have decided to wipe the slate clean and to forgive the hurts inflicted on me. By forgiving, I free myself from the clutches of revenge and hate. I cannot forget, but I can let go of the hurt by saying: the past is the past. I use my experiences to guide me in my future relationships. After all, I am here to learn.

It is much too easy to be overwhelmed with hate when someone hurts you in some way. But hate is a harmful feeling that makes no contribution whatsoever to your well-being. So I let go of the hate and once the emotion has disappeared, I am free and I can grow.

Asking for Forgiveness

"Denying your responsibility when you have harmed someone can only reinforce the feeling of guilt. The best way to find relief is to assume responsibility for your actions, ask for forgiveness and repair any damage you may have caused."
— SHARON WEGSCHEIDER-CRUSE

I am a wonderful being and I am a human being. By making that simple statement and by realizing that I am undergoing a process of discovering and learning, I realize that I can make mistakes. By taking full responsibility for my mistakes and, when necessary, by asking for forgiveness for the harm I have caused, I keep the road to my personal development free of obstacles and guilt. Today, I see that I have the strength and the conviction I need to recognize my mistakes and to ask for forgiveness.

Our Greatness

"The human being is an aspect of the great oneness that we call the universe, with limitations in time and in space. The human perceives his being, his ideas and his feeling as something separate from the rest, a sort of optical illusion of his conscience. This illusion is our prison, limiting our desires and our affection only to those around us. Our task consists of freeing ourselves from this prison by widening the circle of our compassion to embrace all living beings and all of Nature."

— ALBERT EINSTEIN

With time, I have come to understand that goodness and kindness cost me nothing. It is as if I had been afraid of giving, sharing and trusting others. I used to think: "If I'm good, they'll take advantage of me and they'll want more and more from me." This attitude limited my ability to give. I could not give freely, whether it was money, material goods, my time or my love. I realized that my ability to love, to give, and to share knows no limits. At any time I can choose to give or not to give.

Small Steps

"Goodness is more important than wisdom and recognizing this is the beginning of wisdom."
— THEODORE ISAAC RUBIN

Goodness is obvious in great gestures of charity and benevolence, but it is also apparent in the small day-to-day gestures that contribute to the joy and happiness of the people who share our lives. There is no need to sell all we own to go work in a faraway country to experience the miraculous effects of goodness. I can give up my seat on the subway, say hello to a policeman, mow my elderly neighbor's lawn. These small and seemingly unimportant gestures contribute to overall harmony and let us transcend our own interest and reach out to someone else's heart. I can live wisely every day by making the small gestures that contribute to the well-being of others.

Paying Attention to Others

"The nicest gift anyone can give to someone is a deep attention to the fact that they exist."
— SUSAN ATCHLEY EBAUGH

I keep in mind that each person who crosses my path is a spiritual being, a soul that will share my life for a time. My relationships involve human beings, not simply bodies. So when I communicate with someone, I recognize the true being in front of me.

With this recognition, I can behave in a loving and respectful way towards others. I treat them as if they were of very great value. I speak to the true being and not to the personality or the attitude. I don't let others bully me, but I try to act cordially and kindly towards people of all nationalities and all ages.

Serving Others

"No joy equals the joy of serving others."
— SAI BABA

Most of us have lost the notion of serving others. To some extent we associate serving others with a form of degradation or slavery. We live in an age of liberation. But our overly individualistic outlook results in isolation and spiritual hardship. There can only be one true goal for people living within a society: serving others. A lifetime of serving ourselves is sterile and fruitless. A lifetime of serving our families, our communities, our businesses, our companies, our planet is the only true life.

Serving does not mean being a slave or acting as someone else's inferior. Serving means using my talents and my resources for the greater good of all. When I serve, I find self-fulfillment, I create harmony and I become a member of humanity as a whole.

Strength and Weakness

"Through sheer luck, a man may reign over the world for a little while; but by virtue of love and goodness, he can reign over the world forever."

LAO TZU

Many people still don't understand that it is impossible to dominate, control or enslave people using force and aggression. Our societies are increasingly violent and we struggle to settle our differences by using intimidation and violence. Violence breeds violence. Force leads to a reaction of equal magnitude. Such is the structure of the universe. Only goodness, kindness and compassion can tear down the walls that separate us.

Now I see that goodness is the way that leads to the highest levels of consciousness and action. I turn away from intimidation and aggression and I adopt attitudes and behaviour patterns based on love and compassion.

Loving, Learning and Growing

"We who have lived in concentration camps remember people who gave comfort to others, along with their last morsel of bread. Perhaps they are few in number, but they are the proof that you can rob a man of everything save one: the last of human freedoms, the freedom to choose his attitude, regardless of the circumstances, to choose his path."

— VICTOR FRANKL

Now I know that I have the complete choice to live a life of greatness or a life of smallness. I have all the elements in hand to make enlightened choices. I can choose to be good, honest and sincere or I can choose to be selfish, indifferent and superficial. I can choose between the superficial world of appearances or the world of truth and light. I am not here to accumulate material wealth or to honour my physical body. I am here to love, to learn and to grow.

Being a Good Person

"I have kept my ideals because I believe that in spite of everything, the human heart is filled with goodness."
— ANNE FRANK

I know that in spite of what I may have thought or what people may have said, I am good and I am generous. There is no doubt in my mind. Today, I make good and generous gestures. I know that in spite of my mistakes and my failures, I am capable of accomplishing wonderful things. I am a good and generous person.

Sowing the Seeds

"Continue to sow seeds, for you never know which will bear fruit... perhaps all."

— ECCLESIASTES

I no longer doubt the fact that I reap what I sow. It is absolutely impossible to live an unhealthy and dishonest life and not reap the fruits of my actions. Opportunism, greed and dishonesty plunges us directly into darkness and misery. Happiness demands a strong commitment to justice, love and goodness. The human being knows when he is being honest with himself and he know the difference between good and evil. You can live a lie for a time, but in the long run you will no longer be able to live with yourself.

I include my notion of justice and fairness in my actions and I take the straight and narrow road of personal integrity because I am loyal to my inner self.

No Shame

"Humans live by finding refuge in the hearts of others."

— IRISH SAYING

Today, I recognize that I cannot live completely alone. I must accept the help of others who want to keep me safe. I have tried to structure my life in a way that would let me avoid asking others for their support. I have always been convinced that I could take care of everything myself, without the help of anyone else. But now I see the price I paid to establish my independence.

Now I see that there are sincere people who want to contribute to my life and lend me their support. I need not be ashamed of expressing my needs because I know that I too can offer help when someone else is in need. I feel more available to others and more human when I am open to the help and love of others.

Small Anonymous Gestures

"When you are about to do something, even if you are alone and no one else will witness it, ask yourself if you would act in the same way if the whole world was watching, and then act accordingly."
— THOMAS JEFFERSON

I see that I need no recognition other than the simple satisfaction of being fair and good. Of course, there is some merit in giving to charitable causes as a crowd looks on. It sets an example and it shows your intentions to all. But small anonymous gestures of kindness are just as powerful since they shine a bright light where once there was only darkness. The day-to-day difficulties that people experience draw no attention from the media. So if we want to do good, all we need do is go into the street and look with our own two eyes to see where we are needed.

Today, I see that goodness can be expressed daily in simple and often anonymous gestures. These small gestures fill my heart with love and joy.

The Ethics of Giving

"Tenderness and goodness are not signs of weakness and despair, but manifestations of strength and resolve."

— KALHIL GIBRAN

I believe that when I offer something to somebody, I should ask myself certain questions:

1) Does this person really want me to offer one thing or another? Is my gift appropriate and appreciated by the receiver?
2) Do I feel good because I've given something to someone? Does the fact of giving a gift or offering help really make me happy?
3) Is this really the right time for me to give this gift or should I wait for a more appropriate time?
4) Will the offering help or a gift make the other person feel uncomfortable or not?

It is important that I ask myself these questions before offering a gift because my only objective is to contribute to the well-being and happiness of another person. And I have to feel totally comfortable with my gesture.

Being Capable

Today, I know that I am sufficiently strong to hold out a hand and offer my help to someone. I know that I have been lucky and that I am capable of surmounting obstacles in my life. The fact that I am a "capable" individual comes with a responsibility: I must help those sincerely seeking to grow and further their personal development.

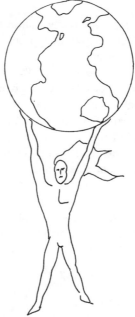

A Tribute to Mothers

Today, I want to pay tribute to my mother and to all mothers. Being a mother is a role that requires an enormous amount of tenderness and goodness. We give mothers almost all the responsibility of sowing the seeds of love, respect and consideration in the hearts of our children.

The role of mothers has been called into question by modern psychology, which looked for the source of all evil in our society in the individual's relationship with his or her mother. These false concepts have only served to create rifts in the family unit. I know that there is no other role as demanding as the mother's role.

Today, I express my deep gratitude and love to all the mothers of the world.

A Tribute to Fathers

Today, the role of fathers is hard to grasp. We ask them to be much more than a model and a provider. We ask them to show the qualities of a mother and a father at the same time and we also tell them that they play a secondary role in the lives of their children. Fathers play a very crucial part in their children's lives. Fathers guide, act as role models, protectors and warriors. Fathers are a child's bridge to the real world.

I pay tribute to fathers and today I know that their role calls for a great deal of courage and determination.

Kind Words

"Kind words can be brief, but their echo resonates forever."

— MOTHER TERESA

A few affectionate words can make all the difference in a person's life. Telling someone that you love them or that you appreciate them can have an important effect on that person. I am generous with my compliments. I tell the people I love that I do love them. I share with friends how important they are to me. I am generous with my kind and loving words.

Going Beyond Limitations

"We are all here to go beyond our initial limitations, regardless of what they are. We are here to recognize our magnificent and divine nature, regardless of what it tells us."

— LOUISE HAY

A barrier is an obstacle that prevents us from achieving a goal or that stops our growth. Life involves all sorts of barriers. But the most challenging barriers are those that we impose upon ourselves. These barriers are hard to jump over because we cannot see them. They are so much a part of our way of thinking and seeing things that they are invisible to us. Throughout our path to self-fulfillment, we must examine the attitudes, perceptions and behavior patterns that hinder our progress. It is only when we can identify our personal barriers clearly that we can find the road that leads to serenity.

Thinking Before Speaking

"If we want to live in harmony, we cannot hurt others in the name of truth. It is important to have the courage to be lucid about our feelings, but it is in our own best interests to think before we speak and to ask ourselves the following question: is this a feeling or am I making a judgment? If it is a real feeling, such as sadness, anger, a sense of rejection, joy, or passion, we must then look for the kindest way to bring attention to how we feel."

— SUE PATTON THOELE

I want to be open and I want to communicate with others. I want to share my feelings and I want to be sincere and authentic. I see that self-affirmation and respect are important. And I also see that it is important to be tactful and diplomatic.

I must prepare my communications. I must be sensitive so that I do not hurt anyone. I must try to express myself by reinforcing the ties of communication. Before expressing myself, I take a few minutes to think and I adjust to the situation at hand.

Gift Giving

I can be myself at all times and under all circumstances. The people around me like me and they are thrilled with the person I am. Being myself does not call for any special effort. Being myself is being spontaneous, it is expressing my feelings without holding back. By being myself, I can experience things and people directly. I live in the present.

Now I understand that the nicest gift I can give to someone else is being the person I truly am. By expressing myself fully, by being present and open, I give others the gift of myself. The key to day-to-day happiness is being myself under all circumstances. What an act of kindness and generosity towards myself and others!

Showing My Greatness

Kindness is a gift we give to others and ourselves. By being kind, I am true to my fundamental nature and reason for living. I know that I can find self fulfillment and the path to wisdom by being kind. I show my greatness, my compassion and my love every day of my life. Being kind brings happiness and serenity into my life.

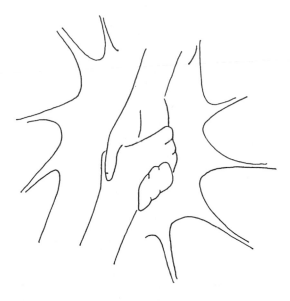

Serenity

Today, I have found serenity and inner peace. At one time I thought that experiencing total well-being, calm and serenity was something impossible. I often had the impression that life was a constant battle to protect myself and to survive. Now I see that inner calm and detachment from the outside world are possible. Serenity comes with spiritual awakening and the recognition of the true nature of beings and things.

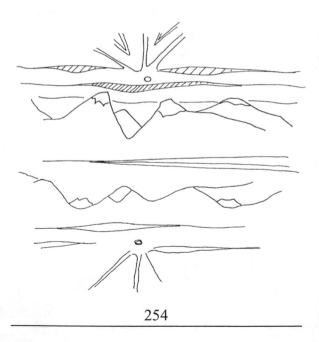

Ethics

I have learned to live honestly, with total authenticity. With time, I have come to understand the importance of honesty, justice and personal integrity This means that I constantly seek to be honest with myself and I set out with the intention of doing good and contributing to the happiness of others.

For me, personal ethics also means success. How can I be faithful to myself and to my principles if I am dependent or if I experience failure after failure? In honest and intelligent work, in the conscious application of my life principles and in the setting of worthwhile goals I see the formula that will inevitably lead me to success.

The Power of My Intentions

Today, I recognize the strength of my intentions and my decisions. I look at the decisions and the fundamental positions I have taken in the past. Were my decisions always wise? I evaluate their appropriateness from today's standpoint. If I am happy with my decisions, I affirm them. If not, I make new decisions.

Living Through Any Experience

I believe that resistance is one of the main sources of suffering. What I resist pursues me and in the end, it catches up with me. So I strive to be open and ready to accept all the experiences that life brings me. This receptive attitude lets me avoid a great deal of trouble because it makes me flexible and capable of adapting to a wide variety of life situations. By being open and receptive, I can handle any situation.

We can react by saying: "I do not want to experience failure, death, old age, violence, hunger, poverty or any other difficult or unpleasant experience." Staying open to all sorts of experiences and all types of communication doesn't mean that we seek out tragedies and problems. Instead, it means that we are prepared to experience them directly should they arise in our lives and we refuse to resist them or run away from them. Today, I am ready to experience things directly.

Eating Well

I know that my health is important and I take the time I need to maintain it. I look at my eating habits and I change those that need changing. I eat healthy foods that give me some of the energy I need each day. I take the time to savor foods by chewing and enjoying every single bite. This makes me more aware of the things I eat and lets me enjoy them to the fullest. By taking the time to eat well, I give my body the resources it needs to stay well and healthy. Eating well is also a sign of great respect for myself. Today, I take the time to eat well. I plan well-balanced menus with plenty of variety. By paying attention to what I eat, I take an active part in improving my health and contributing to my happiness.

Making Scenarios Come True

"You have to accept life as it comes to you, but you should try to make sure that it comes to you in just the way you'd like it."

— GERMAN SAYING

What I want to create in my life is a scenario from my imagination. When my scenario is about to come true, I recognize it because I've already imagined it in detail. And when I begin to move away from making my scenario come true, I can remedy the situation. I turn to my imagination to look at my scenario again. It doesn't matter what my focus is: money, my love relationship, my family, my career. By imagining my scenario, I create a clear vision of the future and I see myself moving forward.

I can strive with all my heart to achieve what I've built in my imagination. I can develop my vision of the future. I can develop a clear vision of the life I want to lead. I can achieve this objective because I can set aside the people and things that prevent me from making my scenario come true.

My Plan of Attack

"You may have habits that weaken you. The secret to change is focussing your energy not on fighting against the past, but on building the future."

— SOCRATES

Today, I am interested in planning. I have understood that to make progress, I must set objectives and I must give myself the means of achieving them. I am completely responsible for my life and the path I travel on this earth. I know what is good for me and for those I love. Today, I will draw up a plan of attack to achieve the objectives that are important to me.

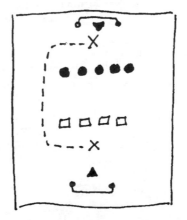

What are my Aspirations?

Today, I remember my aspirations. For a long time, I stopped aspiring to the achievement of my goals and to making my fondest dreams come true. At times I was discouraged, the obstacles in my path seemed insurmountable and gradually, I lost my wings. But the strength within me, greater than life itself, awakened my dreams from their deep slumber.

The Soft Light of Autumn

Today, I let the soft light of autumn caress and warm my skin. I embrace autumn like an old friend who shares wisdom and the fruit of hard labor with me. I let autumn's energy penetrate me and calm my spirit. Today, I take the time to smell autumn's rich, sweet fresh air and I am filled with a sense of calm and tranquillity.

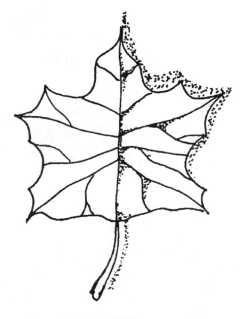

From Dream to Reality

Today, I use my imagination to dream and to look into the future. I know that I create my own destiny. So I use my imagination to create a perfect destiny. Each time I move away from the perfect destiny I have in mind, I make the adjustments required to get back on the right track.

The Joy of Artistic Creativity

There is an inherent joy in artistic creativity. It is a profound form of meditation, a communication with humankind and Nature, between the visible world and the imaginary world. Today, artistic creativity has an important place in my life.

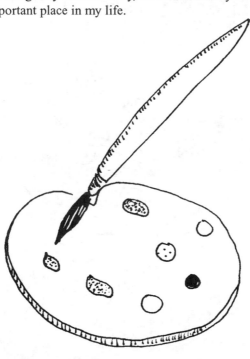

Beauty

Beauty emerges as a superior truth because the spiritual being loves beauty. The spiritual being loves beauty because it sees its own reflection in beauty. When we create beauty around us and within us, we are in close alignment with the divine and noble order of the universe.

Feeling Grateful

Today, I am aware of all the good things in life. I let myself be filled with a feeling of well-being and gratitude for all the opportunities and all the positive experiences that life has given me. I know that real hardship exists and I have experienced it at times; but today, I choose to focus on my good fortune.

I Am Happy

Today, I am happy to be here, to be alive and to be able to breathe fresh air. How fortunate I am to have good health and the ability to move freely and grow. How fortunate I am to have the ability to make my own decisions and to be free to shape my own destiny. How fortunate I am to have the opportunity of proving my worth and finding my own place in this world.

Confusion

Today, I feel that my sense of confusion is fading. Already, I see much more clearly and I am much more confident in my own powers. Now I realize that the confusion I felt was the result of the conflicting messages I have been given all my life. Now I seek my own truth and my own reality. By listening to myself, I feel my sense of confusion fading and disappearing.

Sleepwalking

Today, I am completely awake. Over the years, if we aren't careful, life can gradually put us to sleep it can leave us semi-conscious. Awareness and living in the present both call for a certain degree of effort and willpower. We must refuse the subjective reality that our societies use as a consensus. We must see with our own eyes and hear with our own ears.

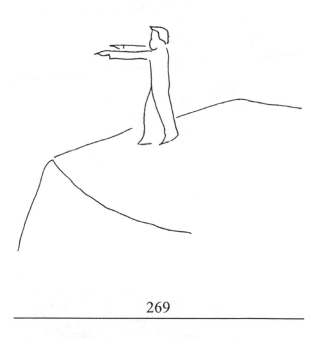

Curiosity

Today, I give in to my curiosity. Curiosity is a completely natural phenomenon. We seek to discover, to understand and grasp the things, events and people around us. So it is natural and necessary to ask questions and to explore.

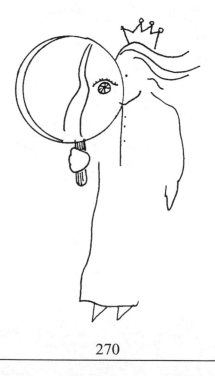

Detachment

Today, I no longer confuse detachment with indifference. I am capable of making decisions when problems occur in my life. I can keep a healthy sense of detachment and my inner calm stays with me under all circumstances.

How to Say "No"

Today, I affirm my own needs by learning to say "No". For a long time I found it hard to express my position clearly and to have my needs recognized by others. I was afraid to displease the people around me and I didn't want to lose their esteem. But now, I understand that when I affirm my own needs and views, people appreciate me more. People who truly value and respect me can understand that at times, I can say "No".

People Like Me

Today, I base my relationships on the principles of mutual help and communication. With time, I have come to see that to be happy, I must establish healthy relationships with others. However, I know that I must be wise when choosing the people I want to share my life with. I also know that it is important to listen and to accept others as they are. I can recognize other individuals who, like me, are working towards self-fulfillment.

Rehabilitation

Today, I have a broader understanding of rehabilitation. We often use the term when referring to repeat offenders and criminals. But in reality, to rehabilitate means to revive and to recover something that was lost. I seek to rehabilitate my joy, my wonderment, my tolerance, my spiritual nature, my creativity. All of these qualities are within me, where they lie sleeping. I need only rehabilitate them.

The Wisdom to Know the Difference

«God grant me the serenity
To accept the things I cannot change,
The courage to change the things I can,
And the wisdom to know the difference.[1]»

Today, I see that there are things I can change. I can create a life that is really worth living. I can live in love and in joy each and every day. I can also learn to accept what I cannot change and to attach less importance to such things in my life.

Each day, I focus on what is important and I let go of the things that are not important. This way, I find serenity in each day of my life.

(1) Prayer adapted from the words of Reinhold Niebuhr.

Gratitude

Today, I am filled with gratitude. In spite of every-thing, my life is a series of wonderful experiences. Each day offers new possibilities, a variety of choices. I am more than a survivor. I am one of the few human beings aware of my inner life and I have chosen the path of love and reconciliation.

I also see that I am fortunate to live in a society that still offers me the possibility of improving myself and expressing myself freely. I can choose my own destiny. I can choose my own vocation. I can create and grow in this society.

Coming Full Circle

"The bitterest tears shed on graves spring from words lost to silence and gestures left undone."
— LILLIAN HELLMAN

Now I see the importance of not giving up on a situation until I do all that is humanly possible. I come full circle and when I finally leave, I leave in peace.

It is sometimes hard to express the feelings I have. I may want to give up on a situation I find difficult before having done everything that can be done. But I know that if I do, the vestiges of the situation can stay with me for a lifetime. When I've given my word, I carry out my commitment by doing what I've promised to do. When I have something important to communicate, I find a way of expressing what I have to say. This way, I can travel through life without a heavy heart.

Finding Balance and Harmony

"Most of our pain and suffering, both physical and emotional, comes from a lack of inner harmony. When we are ill, our immune system works actively to reestablish equilibrium within our organism. In the same way, when we are annoyed, our emotions seek to reestablish harmony."

— SUE PATTON THOELE

In each situation there is the possibility of taking action that leads to inner harmony. In each relationship there is a series of behaviour patterns that leads to communication and to harmony. When I take the time to listen to myself and to do what I must do, I am on my way to inner harmony. Sometimes I must face unpleasant situations. Whenever I do, I stay calm, I listen and I search for ways to achieve the best possible outcome. I am faithful to myself and I refuse to give in to the frustration of the moment. I can find inner harmony each and every day. I embrace painful emotions and then I let them go. I see the ebb and flow in my emotions but I don't let them sweep me away.

The Harmony of Others

Today, I know that I can contribute to the harmony of others. By being sensitive to their preoccupations and by being compassionate, I can guide my words and my gestures. Sometimes, by making small adjustments to how I behave, I can encourage the development of a more nurturing and more harmonious relationship or communication. I accept my role in the happiness of others, regardless of how small it may be. I accept that my words and my actions can have a major impact on others.

Pride in My Accomplishments

"Life is what we make it. This is how things have always been and how they will be until the end of time."

— GRANDMA MOSES

Each day, I have the possibility of accomplishing things. I can accomplish small things, like cleaning my home, or big things, like finishing an important project at work. Each task I accomplish brings me a sense of satisfaction. So I step up my effort to finish my projects and in this way, I spark a sense of pride within myself.

The Harmony in Beauty

"Nature has the gift of healing. It surrounds us with beauty to dress our wounds and revitalize our hearts — as long as we let it. We must get back to Nature, we need to feel the earth under our nails. Even if we live in apartments in the heart of the city, we can grow flowers in pots and their beauty will be a mark of gratitude towards those who water and nurture them. The beauty of the plainest flowers can bring joy to our hearts if we have the courage and the will to contemplate and appreciate them."

— Sue Patton Thoele

When I am in the presence of beauty, my soul quivers. I feel that I am truly alive when I look upon something of great beauty. Nature brings me a sense of calm and inner peace. I go out into Nature to restore my inner harmony. Today, I know that I can find my inner calm when I contemplate the beauty of Nature, when I work in my garden or when I take the time to appreciate the beauty of a flower.

Crying

"Each loss we experience, regardless if it is real or only the threat of a loss, creates in us the need to cry, to mourn and then to move beyond pain since it is associated with suffering. Doing so takes some time. And when we cry over our losses, we grow."
— CHARLES L. WHITFIELD

When I cry, I release the emotions locked within me. So I give myself permission to cry because crying brings me relief and restores my inner calm. I know that by crying, at last I can live my emotions fully and release the feeling bottled up inside me. By crying, I can find reconciliation with my losses and the painful experiences in my life. I am not ashamed of crying because it brings me back in touch with my inner self and it brings reconciliation with the past.

Taking Action Despite Fear

I know that I must face my fears each day. By facing them, I can overcome them. It is completely natural to feel anxious and uncertain when faced with the unknown or with a difficult situation. On the other hand, I must muster my courage and take on the situation. By confronting my fears, I can grow and continue along my life's path to fulfillment. The road to inner harmony is filled with stumbling blocks. But I know that no obstacle, no fear, can ever stop me.

Conquering Time

"Go slowly, breathe deeply and smile."
— THICH NHAT HANH

I can have a determinant influence on time. I realized that I was letting time take control of my life. Time determined my comings and goings. Time determined my quality of life. I had let a system of measurement take control of my life. I saw time acting on me, on my body, on my relationships and on my experience and I had the impression that there was nothing I could do. To some extent, I had to suffer the effects of time and I had to fight against its negative effects.

I have stopped letting time take over my life and pushing me ahead in a race against the clock. I refuse to give in to the constant pressure beating down on me and I focus my attention on the present moment. I have realized that I am in control of time. I can change the way I experience time. I can be free of the negative influences of time.

I Am a Cautious Swimmer

"When you're caught in a ground swell that sweeps you out to sea, there's no use fighting and trying to swim to shore. You have to let go, you have to stop going against the current. When you let go, let the current carry you gently and you can navigate your course and get to shore much more easily."

— A CAUTIOUS SWIMMER

I have realized that applying direct force is rarely useful. Things and individuals seek balance. What is in movement seeks to remain in movement. What is stationary seeks to remain stationary. When I confront something with force or violence, I sometimes fail to take into account the nature and characteristics of that something. It is preferable to observe and to adjust to the situation at hand rather than apply force immediately.

Of course, I can't let events carry me away like a leaf on running water. But by recognizing the nature and cause of a situation, I can develop an approach that is appropriate and positive. I must also recognize the power of my decisions, which can also have a determining influence.

Magic Moment

"If you take a flower in your hand and truly look at it, for just a moment, that flower becomes your entire world."

— GEORGIA O'KEEFFE

In reality, there is only one moment, the present moment. If we waste this moment on thinking about tomorrow or yesterday, it fades away quickly and disappears forever. Here and now, why not resolve to live the present moment to its fullest. I have understood that my resolve must be very strong and very clear if I want to enjoy the present moment at all times.

The greatest pleasures in life are brought to us by the present moment. So I resolve to live in the present moment, here and now.

Living in the Present

"Live in the present. Do all the things you must do. Do all the good things you can each day. The future will open up to you."

— Peace Pilgrim

What I do today, now, will have an effect on tomorrow. I can live in the present moment while sowing the seeds of my successes and my joys in the future. I can live in the present moment and look towards the future with confidence. I can stop time and savor the joys of the moment.

Seeing What is There

"Life is something that happens while we're busy planning something else."
— JOHN LENNON

At times we are so preoccupied with our thoughts and our future projects that we fail to see what it there, in front of our very eyes. At any moment, we have the possibility of reconnecting with our immediate environment simply to see what is in it.

Today, I look through my own eyes. Silently, I look at the world around me in the present moment. When I am with someone else, I take pleasure in being with them genuinely and completely. When I am alone, I take a few moments to reconnect with the present.

The Good Side of Things

Our experience is largely determined by our perceptions. When I focus my attention on the bad side of things, these perceptions have a direct effect on my experience. I cannot be happy if my attention is constantly centered on the negative aspect of life, my job and my relationships. I must check my perceptions before making a judgment. I must seek to look at situations from different angles. This way, in each situation I can develop perceptions that are more accurate.

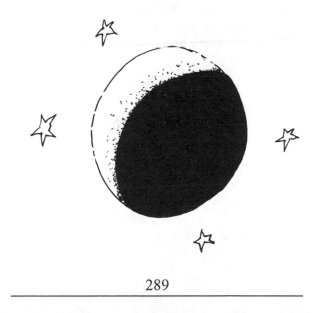

My Natural Abilities

I have natural abilities, things that I do well, almost naturally. When I begin an activity that is very familiar and easy for me, I feel that I am in my element. I enjoy the experience of facility and I am in harmony with myself and with my environment. I feel competent when I undertake this kind of activity. When I express my natural abilities, I feel good and I feel in control.

Today, I will make a list of my talents and my natural abilities. Then I will look at how I can include my abilities in my day-to-day activities. If I have any talent that I don't customarily use, I will find a way to make it a part of my life and to use it more often.

Why Worry?

Worrying is a vague and general feeling of fear, with no specific focus. Worrying is the result of fear of the unknown and a preoccupation with what could happen tomorrow. The only thing I can be sure of is that I am here right now. I have had to face difficult situations and I have overcome them. I will have to face challenges in the future and I know that I have all the capacity and all the resources I need to handle them. When I begin to worry, I tell myself that worrying is useless. I resolve to deal with the here and now and I refuse to try to predict future disasters.

The World According to Me

"We do not see things as they are, we see them as we are."

— ANAIS NIN

I am me and you are you. You have your own perceptions and I have mine. I can appreciate your life experience but I cannot live your life. Of course, you may have a good idea of what my life is like, but you cannot experience it directly. I see the world through my eyes. And you see things in your own way. I see how I create my own life experience based on my attitudes, my thoughts and my actions. I am unique and I see the world according to my own perceptions. You create your life based on your own values, perceptions and behaviour patterns. You are a unique and very worthwhile individual. I am a free and complete individual who brings something totally new to life. You are a very special individual and you carry the richness of your life experience everywhere you go.

Accepting the Unacceptable

"It is extremely hard to accept something that at first glance seems to be unacceptable and for this reason, we should not balk at such a possibility. Letting go of your resistance paves the way to acceptance and serenity."

— SUE PATTON THOELE

At times, we are faced with a situation that we consider to be unacceptable. In such cases we are deeply disappointed and we feel a strong sense of refusal. We are unable to live with the failure, refusal, rejection or loss before us. Our entire being resists the reality of the event in question. This type of experience forces us into areas that we do not want to explore. The truth is that we can handle any experience that life brings us. We can live through anything. Underlying our pain is our resistance to embrace the experience. When, little by little, we begin to face the experience of a new reality, we see that it is possible to include it in our lives and to accept it no matter how hard it seemed at the outset. What I see is that there is no experience that I cannot handle, no reality that I should fear. I am ready for all that life brings me.

The Unexpected

"The strong flames of joy are often lit with unexpected sparks."

— DR. JOHNSON

If I already know how my life will unfold, how can I keep my mind open to new experiences? If I'm content with living exactly the same way I have always lived, how can I build a new life? I am convinced that life will bring me new experiences, new challenges and new possibilities. I seek stability and equilibrium in my life, but I also want to enjoy new experiences. Most importantly, I want to take a whole new look at the world and I want to get to know it from different angles. Today, I am receptive to the unexpected, to surprises. I let people approach me and I am open to new encounters.

Laugh, Dance and Sing Together

"A home where you feel good is a place where parents and children can relax and recover from the pressures of the day. Laughing, singing and dancing are the quickest ways to change preoccupations into celebrations. Having fun together strengthens family ties and encourages honest and harmonious relationships between family members. As they grow up, your children will have a much better chance of feeling comfortable within the family if everyone is having fun."

— JUDY FORD

My original family home wasn't a very nice place to be in. It was often a place of tension and conflict. A place where laughter was rarely heard and where faces rarely seemed happy. I am very aware of what I want to create in my life. I want to live in a happy home where everyone feels safe, where everyone can have fun and laugh. I can create this kind of environment in my own adult life. My family life will serve to calm my soul and restore my trust.

Old Habits

When I recognize a behavior pattern that I don't like in myself, I take the time to choose whether I want to keep that habit. I am not the victim of my old habits. I can choose new behaviour patterns as long as I choose them consciously. Of course, breaking old habits and developing new types of behaviour can require a lot of energy. I know that I have to be patient and loving towards myself and I must reward myself for small victories. I am not chained to the past. Every single day, I decide how to live my life.

Being Receptive

I understand that I must be prepared to receive communications. I listen attentively to others when they want to communicate something to me. Listening means being available to receive a communication. By listening, I show my respect for the person in front of me and I show them that what they have to say is important to me. When they feel that I am listening to them, people are more effective at communicating what they want to say. By listening, I discover a new way to discover others. Today, I resolve to listen attentively.

The Beauty of Imperfections

They say that imperfections make people more likeable. All I can say is that sooner or later, every individual has to face his or her own imperfections and limitations. We can't hope to have every talent, every beautiful trait and every attribute. On the other hand, every person has specific qualities and a unique beauty. Each person has something to offer. And each person has the possibility of improving and growing. We become great when we seek greatness. We are beautiful when we seek to be honest. We are likeable when we let others like us. Everyone has small things that need improvement. And some aren't even aware of their own imperfections.

Being Worthy of Love

For a long time I believed that if I was nice to others, I would be worthy of being loved. Now I see that the truth lies elsewhere. To be likeable or to be loved, I don't have to do anything special. I am worthy of receiving and giving love. I can love myself because I am and because every living being deserves to be loved.

Discovering with My Own Senses

Today, I take pleasure in using my senses. I look, I hear, I smell, I touch and I taste. My senses let me create a link between the physical world and the intangible world. I am tuned into my own senses and I trust them. They are my window on the world and they help me discover it at its best.

My Fundamental Wisdom

One truth is very well hidden by the appearance of things and by the current structure of modern societies which attach more importance to things and to the body, while minimizing the importance of the spiritual being: the ultimate value and importance of our fundamental wisdom and our spiritual life.

Throughout our lives, we receive advice, truths and ideas of all sorts. I listen to others, but I know that I must listen to my own wisdom and to my own ideals as well. The more I develop the ability to listen to myself, the more faithful I will be to myself and the more in harmony I will be with my innate wisdom. Today, I listen to my own wisdom. And by listening to my inner self, I encourage the development of my spiritual life.

Loving Myself

Now I see how my relationship with myself is a determining factor in achieving happiness. The way in which I behave towards myself, the way in which I speak to myself, the opportunities I give myself, the moments of pleasure and relaxation I plan for myself are all very important factors. I used to neglect my own needs and to focus my attention on the needs of others. Now, I see how my relationship with myself is determinant. So I take care of myself. I give myself all the space and all the time I need. I treat myself exactly as I would treat my best friend. I am my own best friend.

Reinventing My Love

I have always believed that I would meet my life partner some day and that from then on, my life would be
transformed into a wonderful adventure. Eventually,
I had to set aside this illusion because I was fundamentally unhappy in my love relationships. I was waiting for the magic moment to change my life. I was
waiting for someone or something better.

True love is a work of love that calls for availability
and commitment. I have to give of myself each day.
I have to reinvent my love each day. This work of love
is based on my commitment, on my word and on my
will to love. Today, I love truly and every day, I
strengthen my relationship by doing things that truly
contribute to it. Sharing your life with someone else
can be difficult and at times, it takes creativity. I am
prepared to work at deepening and strengthening my
wonderful relationship with my life partner.

Opening My life to Love

By opening my heart and my mind to love, I open my life to others. I strive to create a climate of mutual help, communication and tenderness with all those who want to get to know me and to share my life. Of course, when I open my heart to love, I run the risk of being hurt and maybe even of being rejected or disappointed. But the rewards that true love brings are so much more tender and enriching that I accept the risk.

Today, I open my life to love.

Being Free

For me, being free means being free to think my own thoughts, live my own feelings, express my inner self, and communicate with the people I choose to communicate with. Being free also means exploring thoroughly, getting to know something or someone as well as I possibly can. It is having the possibility of saying yes or no, as I choose. It is the possibility of accepting or rejecting something, as I choose. Being free means embracing the joys and hardships of life. Today, I proclaim my freedom. I am free to choose, to accept, to refuse, to advance or to regress. I can make my own mistakes. In my secret garden I grow rich golden wheat that sways in the gentle wind.

Never Truly Alone

I have the profound sense of being guided and being loved. I sense the strength of love in my life. A subtle presence surrounds and envelops me. When I move away from my ideals and my principles, I move away from this loving energy. When I respect myself by being faithful to myself and to my ideals, I invite the energy of love into my life.

Congratulation

"To accept the authentication of our personal value, we must demonstrate modesty only when such a reaction is authentic. When we experience success, we can accept without fear the praise that others give us."
— SUE PATTON THOELE

In the past, I tended to criticize my mistakes and to be very demanding of myself. I easily forgot to compliment myself on my accomplishments. Today, I see that I must congratulate myself each day. I must recognize and compliment myself for my small day-to-day victories. I am a very worthwhile individual. I can be more generous to myself by recognizing and by congratulating myself on my qualities and my accomplishments.

The Fly in the Ointment

By accepting the mistakes and failures of the past and by living the present moment, I free myself from a heavy burden. At times I may attempt to right past mistakes when doing so is possible. But I cannot live in the nostalgia of the past, hoping to recreate events or experiences that are gone. I must connect solidly with the present moment and focus my efforts on carrying out my current projects and plans.

Being Myself

I can be myself at all times and under all circumstances. The people around me, who like and love me, are generally thrilled with the person I really am. Being myself requires no special effort. Being myself means being spontaneous, expressing my inner self, never holding back. By being myself, I experience things and people directly. I live and enjoy the present moment.

I have learned to look at change and improvement as a process that brings me into contact with my inner self. The fundamental being that I am is completely wonderful. As I grow, I remove all the layers that hide my true self from others.

Succeeding

I can succeed on many different levels. I can succeed on the material and financial levels. I can succeed on the emotional level by surrounding myself with a happy and contented family. I can succeed on the professional level by pursuing an interesting career. I can succeed on the spiritual level by achieving higher levels of consciousness and by achieving wisdom and serenity. Success is satisfying. Success gives us full confidence in our abilities and in our determination. Success is noble as long as I do not achieve it at someone else's expense.

Succeeding means being able to actualize the results I imagined. It means reaching my goals and making my dreams come true. It means taking on the challenge of setting things into motion and guiding their movement in the direction I want. Today, I focus my attention on success. I look at my life and I see the many successes I have achieved. I look at the way I achieved my successes and I use the same formula in all aspects of my life.

Personal Boundaries

When we refer to personal boundaries, we refer to the personal place that each individual occupies. We also refer to a person's vital territory, his or her private space and the vital boundaries that serve to protect it.

I am free to choose to share my private space. I can choose who I want to communicate with. I can deny or give access to my private space. Sometimes, when we have been subjected to negative experiences with malicious people, we can withdraw into ourselves and when we do, we refuse all access to our private space. Our personal boundaries are very rigid and exclusive. Conversely, people who have a deep need for approval and love tend to set up very loose boundaries, too easy to break down, and as a result, these people can be hurt. I have evaluated my own personal boundaries and now I give myself the possibility of choosing who will share my privacy and to what extent they will share it with me.

The Principle of Non-Action

There is an ancient book of wisdom written by a Chinese philosopher named Lao Tzu ("Old Master"). The book was written several thousand years ago and it talks about the road to peace and serenity. In his book, the *Tao-ti-Chin*, Lao Tzu outlines the virtues of non-action. Non-action means the ability to wait, to observe, to listen and to explore before acting. Each event is driven by its own dynamics in relation to the laws of the universe. At times, the biggest mistake we can make is taking action instead of letting things take their course. The impatient individual is unable to take the time to explore; he rushes headlong into action and as a result, upsets the natural order of things. There is an important message here. Action must be in harmony with the situation and at times, not taking action and letting events take their course is the best decision.

Consensus

"At poker, you have to be able to win with a losing hand and lose with a winning hand."
— THE FILM "Havana"

The dynamics of poker are much like the dynamics of life itself. If you bet only on winning hands, you spend your time waiting for fate to deal you the ideal hand. But a good player can bet and win with a very weak hand if he manages to convince his opponents that he has a winning hand.

Our success results from our ability to convince others that we're winners. We have to win over those around us if we want to reach our objectives. Winning others over to our side involves no trickery. All it takes is confidence in our own ability to create a consensus on the value of a given project. When the consensus is that the project will be successful, then it will be successful.

Each Person is Important

We are never formally taught that we should be interested in others. However, the sincere interest we have in others can be a determining factor in our life. Each of us is preoccupied by our own fate and most of all, we are aware of our own needs. To succeed, we must show a genuine interest in others. We should look at situations from the point of view that other people may have. We must show that we are sincerely interested in others and their needs. We must resolve to help fill their needs whenever we can and whenever doing so is wise and appropriate.

When I meet people, I try to deepen my relationship with them by asking how they are. I ask about their families, their lives in general. I show an interest in them and I try to understand them.

The Virtues of the Heart

"He who lives for love spreads goodness and compassion all around him. He who ceases to believe in the virtues of the heart becomes a sterile soul, lost and wandering in the desert."

— FRANCIS HEGMEYER

I want to live in a world that is more noble, more generous and more virtuous. A world were goodness, kindness, courage and compassion reign supreme. A world which encourages, celebrates and rewards humility, patience and kindness. I have realized that virtue is not a character trait acquired at birth nor is it a question of education as such. Adopting virtuous behaviour patterns is mainly a question of choice. I decide to adopt specific values and specific types of behaviour. By building a moral framework in my life, I decide to encourage the development of my superior being and I say no to my inferior being.

The Wings of Courage

Courage is an individual's ability to be firm and perseverant in the face of a challenge or of danger. It is the strength and conviction of one's intentions. It is tenacity in the face of uncertainty and difficulty. I have come to understand that courage is a crucial virtue. Without courage, I cannot surmount the obstacles in my path. Without courage, I cannot reach my goals and achieve the dreams that I cherish. So I choose to be courageous. Not because courage comes naturally to me, but simply because I choose to be courageous. I give myself the possibility of being courageous. Today, I give myself the courage I need to climb the mountain that stands before me.

Waiting Calmly

"The most important lesson is life is learning how to take everything calmly."

— MICHAEL FARADAY

Patience — the state of mind of someone who knows how to wait calmly — requires constant work. I have never liked waiting. I have always wanted to reach my goal, find my answer, get whatever I wanted quickly. But today, I have a better understanding of the importance of patience. I must be able to stay comfortable, calm and attentive and I must be able to wait until things happen. Patience isn't a form of torture. Rather, it is a game I play with time. Today, I wait calmly until opportunities come to me.

Becoming an Angel

"Only by giving do we have complete control of our-selves. Anything we are incapable of giving eventually takes control of us."

— ANDRÉ GIDE

Generosity helps humans rise above their own interests, whether they are lasting or temporary interests. By observing, we see the other person and we give them a place in our hearts. Generosity is noble. It lifts human beings to a higher level and gives them virtually angelic qualities. Yes, I can forgive my enemies and those who have harmed and hurt me. Yes, I can rise to a higher level by sharing my time, my property and my intelligence with those who cross my path. Today, I make generosity part of my everyday life and I reach out to those who seek and ask for my help.

Opening My Heart

"The person who does not reflect the image we have of someone who deserves to be loved — the homeless person in the park, the strange character who travels up and down the street on a tricycle decked out in dozens of pennants — is precisely the person who, because he doesn't fit with our preconceived ideas, forces us to broaden our field of vision and our ability to love. See if you can open your heart — not only to those you can give it to effortlessly, but to those who need it as well."

— DAPHNE ROSE KINGMA

When I open my eyes in the morning, and well before I get out of bed, I resolve to do good. My kindness sheds a soft light on the world and makes it more beautiful and a better place to live in. I am the person I want to be when I am kind. I am in harmony with life and I attach great importance to all small gestures and small words and I am kind. When I ask myself to be kind, I am doing the work of angels. When I succeed in being kind, I sense a wonderful inner reward!

Allegiances

Faithfulness, constance in the feelings we have toward ourselves, our principles, our allegiances, our loved ones, all serve as the basis of true love. How can we speak of love, friendship, belonging, and family without also speaking of faithfulness? How can I look at my face in the mirror if I am not faithful to my own ideals, to my own knowledge, to my own principles? How can I ask for respect from those around me when I refuse to embrace faithfulness as a virtue of prime importance? Faithfulness is the cement that keeps relationships together, that seals contracts, that binds families. So warm, so dear and so fragile, faithfulness should be my first promise, my first response, my first idea.

Keeping My Word

"What we do today, at this very moment, will have a cumulative effect on all our tomorrows."
— ALEXANDRA STODDARD

With my words, I invent who I am, I create who I am and I create the reality around me. My word is all that I really have in this world. When I give my word, I give my honor, my commitment and I share all the strength of my intentions and my mission. When I break my word, I betray myself profoundly and I waste my strength. Now I understand the importance of respecting my word. It is a question of honor and personal integrity.

Someone Else's Shoes

Freedom and tolerance are so closely linked that one cannot exist without the other. How can I be free if I cannot recognize the freedom of others, if I cannot tolerate differences? Tolerance is a synonym for generosity. Tolerance cannot be imposed by law or by force. I can choose to be tolerant and to respect the differences I see around me. I can let people be who they are. Tolerance can only be enriching and stimulating in my life. Today, I am tolerant because in my eyes, tolerance is the first expression of social intelligence.

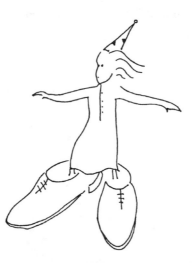

Consideration

"Giving money isn't enough. Money isn't enough: money can always be found. What the poor really need is love from your heart. Spread love wherever your path takes you!"

— MOTHER TERESA

Consideration should reign in our cities, in our communities and in our families. By being considerate, I recognize that I belong to a particular group, I recognize that each member of the group is my brother and he is a full-fledged member of my family. I cannot accept the fact that consideration could disappear from a small corner of the world or from the planet as a whole. By being considerate in my day-to-day life, I create ties of friendship and affection and I make the world a better place.

A Little Further

Perseverance, the ability to push on, to clear the way to the top, to say no to the reflex that urges me to give up, will always be useful in enterprises that are truly worthwhile. I can achieve all of my objectives. I can make all of my dreams come true. I can experience all that life brings me. And perseverance is the key. When the weak and the lazy have fallen by the wayside a long time ago, I will embrace the mission of continuing to the end, even when I am hurt and hungry. Perseverance holds within it the fruits of success.

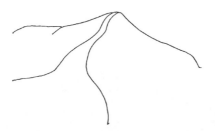

Messengers of Love

"Joy is love exalted, peace is love repose; long-suffering is love enduring; gentleness is love in society; goodness is love in action; faith is love on the battlefield; meekness is love in school; and temperance is love in training."

— DWIGHT L. MOODY

We are inspired to hear about the works and lives of certain brillant beings: Mother Teresa, Gandhi, Jesus Christ, Mohammed, L. Ron Hubbard, Martin Luther King Jr., to name just a few. These very outstanding beings touched us so deeply with their message of love, tolerance and hope in the human race that they singlehandedly altered our perceptions of life and love. We can use their message of love to further enhance our own lives and the lives of those around us. There is, in each and everyone of us, the potential to love and to build with love, to spread peace, hope and tolerance with our deeds and words. We can, in our everyday life, be messengers of love.

The Superior Being

"The Latin word agape signifies understanding and redemptive goodwill towards all men. It is an overflowing love that expects nothing in return. Theologians would say that it is the love of God that governs the hearts of men. When one loves in this way, one loves all men — not for themselves, but because God loves them."

— MARTIN LUTHER KING JR.

When I choose to develop my superior being, I choose to develop what is noble, generous and magnanimous in me. I say no to the gratification of the moment and I say yes to justice and to beauty. I can be great. I recognize the moment when I rise to a higher level of functioning and when I abandon my need to be right and to win. I recognize the moment when I choose to develop the good in me and when I go beyond my own limitations to achieve greatness. Some situations require that I set aside a particular position or point of view and that I act in a more generous and more noble manner. When I go beyond my limitations in this way, I awaken the superior being within me. I embrace the greatness in my life and I become a very different person.

Being Genuine

"Strength is expressed through ferocious honesty with oneself. Only when one has the courage to face things as they are, without illusion or deception, can the light of truth spring forth to guide us on the right path."
— THE I CHING

Honesty, the ability to see and say things as they truly are, is the key. How can I find my rightful place in this world if I am not honest with myself? How can I build lasting relationships and friendships if I am not honest with others? How can I be happy when I refuse to abandon myself completely to truth? Those who choose lies and deception can experience power for a certain period of time, but sooner or later, they become the victims of their own machinations. By embracing the virtue of honesty, by making an ever-lasting pact with truth, I give myself the opportunity to be, to grow and to live happily and without regret. Today, I know that by being honest with myself and with others, I create a moral framework that protects me, nurtures me and helps me rise above petty games.

Spreading Harmony

"Our lives are punctuated with kind words and gracious gestures. We feed on expressions marking basic courtesy, such as: "Excuse me, please." Impoliteness, the negation of the sacrament of consideration, is yet another characteristic of our society, focused on money, deprived of spirituality, perhaps even deprived of the pleasure of living."

— ED HAYS

Kindness is easy to include in the way I interact with the people I encounter in my day-to-day life. I can be kind to those who cross my path. By being kind, I create harmony around me, I recognize that the people around me are important and I show them my respect and my love. People react more positively to kindness. They want and look for kindness in all of their interaction with others. Kindness opens the heart and the soul. It enables communication and affection to emerge and flourish. By being kind, I sow the seeds of love and harmony.

A Small Particle of Divinity

"Forgiving is looking at the person who has offended you in a totally different way. Through the eyes of charity and love. It's a hard thing to do, but it can change a life. Because forgiveness breathes new life into a relationship and changes the chemistry between two people — from bitterness to tenderness."
— DAPHNE ROSE KINGMA

I have learned to forgive because in forgiveness, there is a small particle of the divine. Forgiveness is noble and good. By forgiving those who have offended or hurt me, I let love into my heart. I let bitterness and anger fade away and I choose the path of compassion. I forgive simply for the sake of forgiving. I do not forgive because I have been told that forgiveness is good. I forgive because forgiveness brings me back into contact with my core, it lets me focus my attention and my effort on something else. I haven't got the time nor the wish to maintain negative thoughts. I want to be free, so I forgive — forgiveness sets me free.

Small Gestures

"Thoughtfulness, that most wonderful of products of the human heart, expresses itself most effectively in small gestures."

— MARY BOTHAM HOWITT

Politeness and courtesy were invented to make the world a gentler, more beautiful and more wonderful place. Courtesy takes only a few seconds and it involves very simple gestures: taking time to say hello to someone; letting someone go ahead of you when you're waiting in line; giving up you seat on the bus. You don't have to be rich to be courteous. Courtesy is simple and it fills my heart with a small and discreet kind of joy. Today, I will be courteous with all those who cross my path. Being courteous makes my happy.

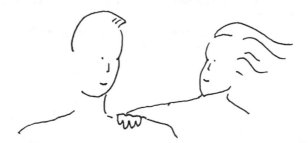

Taking Someone's Hand

"Perhaps a voyage is less a voyage in time or a voyage in space and more a voyage in presence. The greatest distance we can travel is the distance that separates us from a person who is close to us."

— NELLE MORTON

I can let others touch my life. I can be present and sensitive to the needs, feelings and difficulties of others. Because I am a human being, I can recognize that others share the same types of experiences that my life has brought me. Compassion isn't something passive. I must react and come to the aid of those reaching out to me. Sometimes, compassion requires only a tender and understanding look. Sometimes, it requires more. Above all, it requires the ability to walk in the other person's shoes so that I can understand and share with them.

A Gracious Heart

For me, graciousness means many things. Being gracious means being able to give and to receive simply, with no ulterior motives. Being gracious means being generous and giving more time, more space or the benefit of the doubt to someone. Being gracious means keeping your head high in all situations, using your power of discernment and detachment despite the circumstances. Being gracious means moving ahead without fanfare, without trampling on anyone or anything, paying attention to the sensitivity of others and respecting their life experience. This definition is only partial, but it conveys the basic desire to be generous, respectful and cordial to others by behaving courteously, diplomatically and honorably.

Today, I resolve to be more gracious because graciousness is a quality that leads directly to self-esteem and harmony with others. By being gracious, I can go from one situation to another with dignity and honor. By being gracious, I can give and I can receive freely. I can let others help me and love me. I can give help to those who cross my path.

The Light of Discernment

Discernment is the ability to make sound and clear judgments. It is a valuable tool in my work to achieve personal development and spiritual growth. How can I tell the difference between good and evil without discernment? How can I see the truth in events without the piercing light of discernment? How can I surround myself with healthy and helpful people without discernment? Discernment is something I can develop. When I listen to myself and when I am receptive to the messages that come from my inner self, I can choose and act with discernment. Sometimes I have to take a break, say a prayer or meditate before I can awaken to my discernment. But taking time out is always worthwhile because discernment is a powerful asset that I can use to make fair and enlightened choices.

I have a profound knowledge of life within me. My profound knowledge comes from my discernment. Today, I will listen to my inner wisdom and I will make my choices with discernment.

Gentleness

"I believe that humanity will not only last, it will prevail. Man is immortal, not because of all creatures, he is the only one with an indefatigable voice, but because he has a soul, a spirit capable of goodness and compassion."

— WILLIAM FAULKNER

Gentleness will always be more piercing, more penetrating than brute force. Just as water shows its strength in the fact that it has no resistance but can still grind stone into sand, the greatest victories are won with gentleness. Gentleness lets me tame and eliminate all resistance. By being gentle, I let things and individuals come close to me and I touch them deeply.

Today, I pay tribute to gentleness. I put down my weapons and I adopt gentleness in my everyday life.

Simplicity

"All we need to feel happy we can find here and now: a simple heart."

— NIKOS KAZANTZAKIS

When we adopt a sound lifestyle and apply sure values such as respect, compassion, consideration and honesty every day, life becomes much simpler.

When I give freely and when I set out with the intention of doing good, how can I fall victim to depression and anxiety? If I am faithful to my principles and tenacious in the face of adversity, how can I stray from my objectives? Most of the problems facing me cannot withstand my piercing gaze. I am the author of all that I feel and all that I experience. So how could I ask a stranger what I should think and how I should live my life?

Competence

"It is not by doing things we like, but by liking the things we do that we can discover life's blessings."
— JOHANN VON GOETHE

I define competence as the ability to carry out a project or a task efficiently, in such a way as to achieve superior results. Basically, this virtue is the result of a commitment to excellence and the capacity to give our all to our work and to our vocation. Competence inspires respect and admiration because it is a form of esthetics, the beauty that we find in the work of a craftsman, a true professional, a dedicated soul. I believe that competence is a virtue that we acquire when we truly want to serve and help others, when we are proud of our work and when we aim at perfection. Competence fills the individual with pride and self-esteem and it gives him a certain degree of power, as well as the possibility of making a difference in the lives of those he touches. I bring competence to my professional life. I give my all to my work and I constantly seek to improve my abilities. I love my work and I love myself because I do my work well.

Honoring My Commitments

We all look for those rare individuals who honor their commitments. We can rely on such people at all times and we can count on their support in difficult times. Being worthy of trust is not an innate quality, it is acquired with wisdom and is part of the fundamental values that a person decides to adopt or decides to reject.

Honoring commitments is a superior virtue that combines courage, discernment, responsibility and justice. We honor our commitments when we know that our word carries weight, when we are faithful to ourselves and our principles and when we attach a great deal of importance to the nature of the relationships we build. To be worthy of trust, we must choose our principles ahead of our own interests.

I honor my commitments. When I build ties of friendship, I am ready to support that person to the very end. My close ones, my friends and my associates know that they can count on me.

Goodness

Each day, we hear of senseless acts of violence. We are increasingly insensitive to such phenomena, living in the hope that we and our loved ones will not be random victims. Although we have very little understanding of the specific cause of gratuitous and perverse violence, we know that drugs, poverty and the State's progressive disengagement in the areas of health and welfare seem to have a stronger and stronger effect on the mental health of individuals. During times of chaos, people of good will must act together to counter the harmful effects of violence with unbelievable gestures of goodness, compassion and humanity. We cannot succeed if we focus on ourselves or if we fight violence with violence. Today, I take on a large part of the responsibility we all have for the world we live in. I choose to get more closely involved with my community by doing volunteer work and helping those who may be less fortunate than I am.

Magnanimity

Magnanimity is found in the great souls who show mercy and benevolence towards the weak and the less fortunate. Magnanimous individuals can forgive insults and imperfections because they see the inner self of others. They are good and they spread kindness wherever they go. I have never though of myself as magnanimous. But I can aspire to acquiring this virtue. For the moment, I am still preoccupied with certain considerations but I foresee the day when I will live freely and sow the seeds of love and kindness with each of my words.

Where Have All the Flowers Gone?

"When I was in high school in the sixties, I began to see the world around me changing. I really got into the flower power revolution and believing that we could change the world for the better. In retrospect, maybe we viewed life and society in a somewhat simplistic way, but I know we had our hearts in the right place."
— ANONYMOUS

After the pop psychology of the seventies came the hard edged economic ideology of the eighties and nineties. Today, we measure the economic value of things and of relationships and easily forget the human and spiritual aspects of life. Viewing life in economic terms cannot bring us peace and happiness. Dealing with our friends, families and associates in economic terms will not bring us closer to truth and beauty. There are certainly real economic factors in life that must be considered but ultimately, we must confront the fundamental issues; Am I happy? Are my friends, family members and associates happy with me? Am I having fun? Are those around me having a good time of it? What can I do to make the world a better and a safer place for me, my family and friends? These are not questions of economics but rather questions of the heart.

Saving

"The poor seek riches and the rich seek heaven, but the wise man seeks tranquillity."

— SWAMI RAMA

Saving — the art of managing financial resources by avoiding frivolous or needless expenses — is surely a virtue. It takes a great deal of wisdom to use the resources we have on hand judiciously because the outside forces that encourage us to spend and to consume are very strong. Only those who succeed in managing their resources wisely can achieve a higher level of freedom and self-determination. The virtue of saving is not something found in greedy, penny-pinching people. It is the wise and judicious use of resources to conserve them and to make them grow. Resources invested in a company to develop its products are part of the virtue of saving.

Today, I look at my situation and I identify the types of behavior that lead to saving. I look for ways to make my resources grow because I know that this will help me achieve a higher level of freedom and self-determination.

Moderation

Temperance is a virtue that enables us to recognize the danger of excess, the danger of extremes. When individuals give in to one pleasure in particular, they risk being trapped by that pleasure and falling victim to it. We all know individuals who fall into excess. Their life is sheer hell. Their lives are filled with suffering and illusions.

I have experienced the consequences of excess as well and I have paid its price. Today, I embrace temperance because I have found my equilibrium once again. Temperance is sobriety, it is the clarity of mind to see that the flesh is weak and that I cannot grow and live happily in a world of excess.

The Openness of Children

As we live through the sometimes difficult experiences that life brings us, little by little we can choose to withdraw into ourselves. As years and experience go by, we can focus on ourselves and we can experience more and more difficulty in being open to others and in living life fully. There can be no doubt that keeping an open mind is a virtue because life is filled with events and situations that encourage us to shy away from others. Only very determined individuals can resist the trend by keeping an open mind to creative experiences.

When we look at young children, we see the fundamental nature of openness. For children, life is a creative experience. They touch, taste, question and bring a sense of wonderment to the things and situations they encounter. Because children's minds are always open to new experiences, they live through the whole gamut of emotions, finding the joy of discovery in the end.

I can have the spontaneity and joy for life that children have. I can be open to others and to different experiences. After experiencing disappointment, I can quickly move on to something else and return to an openness, a willingness to play and have fun.

343

Indulgence

"The quality of indulgence cannot be faked; it falls on our heads like the gentle rain from heaven; its blessing is twofold; it blesses he who gives it and he who receives it."

— WILLIAM SHAKESPEARE

Indulgence stems from our capacity to see the larger picture and to recognize our responsibility to humanity as a whole. No creature escapes the body of love, compassion and responsibility that is indulgence.

I have not achieved the level of consciousness, responsibility and love needed to exercise perfect indulgence, but I am preparing the way by showing indulgence in my everyday life. By being generous, sincere and helpful, I show my indulgence. I have a very open mind. I can share my good fortune with those around me or with those who simply happen to cross my path.

My dreams

"With both feet on the ground, you can't learn much about free falling."

— JOYCE MAYNARD

I believe that if I didn't have dreams, my life would be dull and routine. And furthermore, if I have no dreams, how will I know if I am getting any closer to my ideal life? Where will I find the inspiration to carry on and to build a better life?

Today, I nurture my dreams. Today, I let my imagination run wild and I see my ideal future before my very eyes. This ability to create my own dreams gives me hope and inspiration each day. I know that the pleasure lies not in the realization, but in the building of my dreams and in the road that I travel to make them come true.

Dreaming means taking risks because a dream that involves no action is simply an illusion. So each day, I work at making my dreams a reality. For me, there can be no other way to live.

Today, I dream and I look for ways to make my dreams come true.

Hand Made

"I'm a window washer and I have a special affection for the windows I wash. I am familiar with their individual personalities, their mineral deposits, their bad joints and the holes they've gotten from lead pellets. I remove the smallest traces left behind by bees and the vestiges of the visits that flies and birds pay to "my" windows and I eliminate any damage done by paint. I bring along garden shears and I cut back the shrubs and plants that dare to interfere with my windows. As I tour the premises, I get a great deal of satisfaction when I see my windows gleaming in the sun."

— **ANONYMOUS**

Today, I see that when I work with my hands, I find inner harmony. By doing simple work, my life itself becomes simpler and easier. Worries disappear and I find joy and happiness.

Seeing Beyond

Appearences can be deceiving. A failure may be a victory if you know how to learn from it. A rejection may be an opportunity to move on to something else. The end of one relationship marks the start of a new relationship. Change is omnipresent in our lives. We should never cling to any one situation. Instead, in the end of an experience, we should see the beginning of something new.

When I embrace the natural cycle of birth, growth, decline and death, I do not see death as an end, I see it as a beginning. Once the darkness has eliminated the last light of dusk, not long after, it must give way to the first glimmer of dawn. I need not fear the darkness. It brings with it the seeds of light.

To Choose or Not to Choose

We are constantly asked to give, to participate, to buy and to sell. We should keep in mind that we have our own projects, our own objectives, our own ambitions. We are completely free to choose whether or not we want to participate.

I can say yes, I can say no, I can say maybe, or I can say that I can't decide right now. I have a whole range of possibilities to choose from. And I keep in mind that I have my own priorities. Today, I know that I am free to choose and I am equally free not to choose.

Each Moment is New

Today, I know that each moment brings with it new possibilities, a new window on the world. Each moment of my life, I live to see the beauty around me and to contribute to making the world beautiful in my own way.

Today, I know that each moment brings renewal. I take pleasure in the fact that all things change. Everything is in a constant state of transformation. I will not try to resist the current of change and I will follow the gentle flow of transformation.

The Fountain of Youth

Oh! Which of us wouldn't love to drink from the Fountain of Youth and stay eternally young? Perhaps after decades and centuries in this body, I could achieve my ideal life, I could find my ideal mate, visit every beautiful place on earth and conquer the world. But how long would it take before I got tired of such an existence? One hundred years? Two hundred years? Three hundred years? After all this time alone with myself, wouldn't I want to leave everything behind and find paradise and my final resting place? On second thought, I don't believe I would drink from the Fountain of Youth because I love this dance of birth and death. It gives me all the time I need to discover who I am and where I am going.

The Need for Consolation

Many of us have to carry burdens that are often to heavy to bear; we have problems and sorrows that bring us pain. And that pain and hardship can seem unbearable. When we recognize this fact, we recognize that many of us need consolation. In the face of tragic events, we offer consolation.

Today, I refuse to abandon my friends. I extend my hand. I know that when I console someone's pain and sorrow, I feel the positive effect of consolation myself.

Critical Parents

There comes a time in life when we refuse to hear criticism. We refuse to hear the sermonizing words that explain how we should live our lives. We live our lives as we choose. Even children are not very receptive to criticism and punishment. Of course, they can be afraid of critical parents who threaten punishment, but the genuine individual does not react to criticism and guilt. The genuine individual seeks encouragement, support, friendship, love and constructive advice. When faced with criticism, we withdraw. Critical parents constantly complain and instill guilt but they get very few results. This is why I am not a critical parent with myself or with others. Criticism never works. Today, I give myself encouragement and I surround myself with true friends.

The Answer is Within

"We always find what we look for. The answer is always there and if we give it time, it will reveal itself to us."

— THOMAS MERTON

Through prayer or quiet contemplation, we always find the answers to our questions. When we ask a question, we set off a profound process of interrogation in our souls. The soul, our true self, will search for and find the answer. The answer may come to us in our dreams, in the way in which events unfold or in a deep sense of intuition. We all have access to our inner wisdom at all times. All we need do is ask our question and wait patiently for the answer.

Deserving Respect

"No one can make you feel inferior without your consent."

— ELEANOR ROOSEVELT

Sooner or later, we all realize that some people fail to give us the respect we deserve. It can happen to anyone. For some people, showing a lack of respect is a means of self-affirmation. Rather destructive, this approach serves only to create the illusion of control and superiority. In such instances, it may seem that there is nothing we can say or do to change the way in which this person treats us. They seem to find nothing to like about us. And often, they continue to show their disrespect to the point of making us angry. On the other hand, other people can show a lack of respect, realize it and apologize for their behavior. Very early in any discussion, we realize what type of person we are dealing with. In both instances, confrontation is useless. We should simply draw the person's attention to his or her transgression or end the discussion.

Today, I demand respect. If people show a lack of respect, I try to rectify the situation. If there is no change, I keep away from these toxic relationships.

A Wonderful Being

Now, I let my natural goodness shine through. Goodness creates places of joy and freedom in our lives. By being good, I rise above the fight for survival or the struggle to accumulate material wealth. I live consciously to create a better world for everyone.

When I assert who I am fundamentally, I am in touch with my essence. More and more, I seek to express the essence within me. Gradually, I peel away all the layers hiding my true self, I shed all the things that are not truly me and I discover the beautiful and wonderful being that I am.

Living Together

Living together, sharing your life with someone, implies the deep desire to communicate with that someone and to participate actively in his or her development. We all know that we can live with someone without ever building a true relationship, we can share space without ever being on the same wavelength. A relationship is genuine when there is no distance between the two partners, when each can feel what the other feels, when each can share the other's aspirations and cherish them as his or her own. Such closeness and such a blurring of boundaries can be difficult at times. But we can share our lives without losing the sense of our own individuality. This is the challenge in any love relationship: living side by side with someone without asking or expecting them to be like us.

Choosing Our Burden

"Freedom is choosing your own burden."
— HEPHZIBAH MENUHIN

At one point, I came to understand that I had to serve a cause. I had to choose one side or the other. I could not stay on the fence much longer. I could choose between serving my own interests and ignoring injustices, lies and the suffering of others or I could serve my brothers and sisters by shedding the light of my own awareness on the world around me. I have chosen to shoulder my responsibilities to my family, my community and the human race because ultimately, I have realized that this path is easier since I will not feel the need to fight against my convictions.

Healthy and Lasting Relationships

"No bed is big enough for three."
— GERMAN SAYING

My relationships must be healthy. This means that each person involved in the relationship must work at making the relationship enjoyable and fulfilling. By communicating my feelings frankly, I give the other person an accurate picture of how I see the relationship. The more the communication between the two of us is clear and honest, the more chances the relationship has of lasting and growing, in an context of love and understanding. A relationship is like making fresh bread each morning. The right amount of yeast and well kneaded dough, an oven heated to the right temperature and an exact cooking time results in a wonderfully delicious loaf of bread that we're happy to share. In the case of a relationship, by communicating my feelings and demonstrating my love, by respecting the other person for who they are and by listening carefully when they speak to me, I enable the relationship to grow and last.

Today, I give myself the right to live in a healthy and lasting relationship. I work to make the relationship a success. I resolve to create relationships where love, communication, feelings and my true self can express themselves freely and unconditionally.

Wanting What You Already Have

"Happiness isn't getting what you want, it's wanting what you have."

— ANONYMOUS

There's a little secret to living happily every day: wanting what you already have! This concept may seem a little crazy in a society that claims that happiness increases as we accumulate more and more material wealth. But many people now realize that this equation is completely false. Happiness has nothing to do with consumerism.

The conviction that we have to consume to be happy inevitably throws us into a spiral of constantly unanswered wants. On the other hand, to break out of this vicious circle, an individual can choose to be happy with what he or she already has. Each of us can choose to be content with what we have.

A World With Imperfection

Yes, the world is filled with imperfection. But what would I do in a perfect world, sitting on my little cloud and strumming my harp all day long? The way things stand now, there's a great deal left to do, many things to improve and many dreams to make come true. Yes, our societies are filled with imperfection. But still, I am happy and I see the things that I can do. I consider myself lucky to be living in this era, in this world and I accept the challenges it brings me.

Today, I rejoice at imperfection because I know that I can do something to make the world a better place.

Serving Others

"Life teaches us that the only worthwhile endeavor is serving others."

— LEWIS CARROLL

Today, I choose to serve others. I see that life is fuller and richer when I give of myself and when I am open to serving others. I am not here for myself alone, I am here to contribute to the happiness of others. When I help someone, I fulfill my divine mission. When I serve someone, I advance on the road to happiness and serenity.

Extraordinary Goodness

"When we don't like the world we live in, there is always the option of creating the world we want through acts of goodwill."
— MELADEE AND HANOCH MCCARTY

We all have obligations. And simply by being responsible in fulfilling our obligations, we contribute to the order of things. No one can criticize us or resent us for being a responsible father, a good mother, a competent worker, a reliable colleague or a dedicated teacher.

But when we move outside the framework of our day-to-day responsibilities and outside our immediate circle to make spontaneous and gratuitous gestures of kindness, our life becomes an extraordinary contribution to the world.

Few people can lay claim to making extraordinary gestures of good. But there is a sphere of actions that lies beyond the daily, that goes beyond the ordinary and that vibrates with compassion and love. We all have the possibility of entering this sphere.

The Pleasures of the Soul

"We take little pleasure in taking medicine, but pleasure itself happens to be a very good medicine."
— JOSH BILLINGS

Today, I embrace the simple pleasures of life. I reward myself for all the good work I do throughout the year. I congratulate myself on the fine person I am and for the progress I have made in recent months. Today, I will give myself a gift and I will thank myself for being patient and for the love I show others. I know that I can spoil myself a little today, so I will take part in the activities I enjoy the most.

Respecting Differences

Today, I embrace my differences and those of others. Difference and diversity are fundamental to two things: the adventure and recognition of beauty. Difference lets me explore and discover new experiences and new territories. Difference is a source of fascination and great beauty. When I see something different and original, I am attracted and fascinated by its difference. Today, I know that my eyes and my soul search for difference and that difference searches for me. I am happy knowing that before me lies a world of differences to discover and explore.

Recognizing a Rainbow

Today, I can see the small rainbows around me and I can recognize them as God's messages. I see them in the faces of my loved ones, in the dawn's early light, in the eyes of my dog as he greets me at the door, in the song of the birds in my backyard tree. I am open to receiving these small, very discreet and very personal messages of love. I marvel at the simplicity and the beauty around me. I let small daily miracles work magic in my life.

Creating a Rainbow

If I have eyes to see the rainbows around me, I also have the heart and the hands to create rainbows. I place them here and there on my path, for others to discover them and so that they too can marvel at the beauty in life. I write small love notes and I leave them on my partner's pillow, I bring flowers to my elderly neighbor to celebrate the holiday season, I tell a colleague that I can watch the office so she can get her shopping done, I volunteer to help out at a blood drive. Today, I create my own rainbows and I use them to express God's love in my own way.

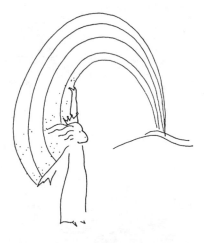

Finding Support

We have all lived through times when we needed support. There is nothing shameful or abnormal in needing emotional or financial support. We have been conditioned to believe that asking is a form of humiliation and defeat. But the truth is entirely different. There is a form of nobility and honesty in asking for help. Like many other people, I have experienced hard times, where money was scarce. I was so stubborn, I didn't want help from anyone. But with time, I realized that each of us can offer and ask for help. Today, I give you my support. Tomorrow, you'll do the same for me. And should I never need your help, then you will have the opportunity of helping someone else instead.

Coming to the Rescue

I believe that in each family, there is a solitary soul who wants to celebrate the holiday season alone. He or she is unable to admit that the holiday season is a difficult time, but silence can be eloquent. Of course, we should not pass judgment. But we can take the time to tell the person that we love them and they are welcome in our home during the holiday season and all year long. The solitary soul may choose to refuse to join in the celebrations, but he or she will be touched by our good intentions and our loving wishes.

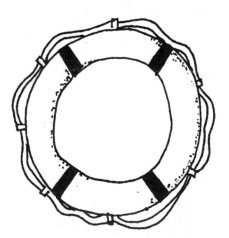

Reconciliation

"There is no remedy for love, beyond loving even more."

— HENRY DAVID THOREAU

Christmas is a day of family celebrations. A day devoted to love and remembering the birth of Jesus Christ. For many people, this is a magical day because it fills their hearts with joy and tenderness towards their loved ones and humanity as a whole. For others, Christmas Day is extremely difficult because it awakens painful memories of the past, broken relationships and broken families, deep disappointments and loneliness. As Christmas draws near, these people become sadder and more and more anxious. Excited or terrified, no one is indifferent to the one day when the entire world stops to celebrate. Because we are keenly aware of the suffering of others at this time of year, we see many charitable and benevolent gestures. Today more than any other day, the world needs gestures of compassion and kindness. I can't be indifferent. I must go out to look for ways to come to the aid of others. So many people need help and there are so many ways to help.

Weariness of the Soul

I believe that we sometimes confuse emotional suffering with a weariness of the soul. When the soul cannot express itself, when it cannot assert its existence or when it is not nurtured, the result can be pain. But the pain is not emotional although it may be associated with emotions. It is a weariness of the soul. It isn't easy to heal a weary soul. The soul, our true being, seeks to manifest itself but finds no means of expressing itself in the day-to-day life of the individual. It is a question of awareness.

Once we determine that we are suffering from weariness of the soul, we must search for an answer to our discomfort. Each individual will find a specific way to respond to weariness of the soul: prayer, art, reading, becoming part of a support group, etc. Various approaches exist and some are more effective than others, but each individual must decide on the best approach to restoring equilibrium.

A Moment Can Change a Life

"There are people who leave a mark on our lives, even if for only one moment. And after that moment, we are never the same. Time has no importance, but certain moments are important forever."

— FERN BORK

As I looked back on my life, I realized that certain decisions, certain encounters, certain meetings and certain events were extremely determinant in my personal growth. These crucial moments profoundly changed the course of my life. A few moments to change an entire life! A few minutes to change me forever! Such moments, so precious and so rare, happen or are created by us, and stand at crossroads in our lives. Today or tomorrow, one of these wonderful moments may occur in my life. And I will be faced with an important decision that will mark my existence until the end of my days. Therefore, I resolve to be open to this most amazing of all moments that I have the opportunity of spending here with you.

The Virtues of Error

"Children aren't afraid to try new things; they aren't afraid of failing or of trying again. So why are we, as adults, so obsessed with failures — our own and those of our children? Why is it so hard to let our children be average, to let them make mistakes? Why do we feel so much anxiety as soon as we make a mistake?"

— JUDY FORD

We believe, perhaps unconsciously, that we should always succeed and look good in every situation. This belief limits our ability to succeed because it makes it difficult for us to recognize and accept our mistakes. Furthermore, the need to succeed at all costs hinders our ability to act freely and spontaneously.

Today, I give myself the freedom to act and I am prepared to accept my mistakes. I know that if I make a mistake, I can recognize it and I can adjust my future behaviour. I see that spontaneity and freedom of action are more important than appearances.

Taking Stock

"When we set aside all that is impossible, we see that what is left — as hard as it may be to believe — is where we can find Truth."

SIR ARTHUR CONAN DOYLE

Today, I take stock of the year that is drawing to an end. I look at things coldly to see if I am truly happy and if the choices I have made led me in the right direction. I conduct a detailed moral inventory and I see what good things I have accomplished and the harm that I may have caused. If I have caused any harm, I look for ways to make amends. I also make a list of the things that I want to accomplish in the coming year.

Prepare My Heart for New Things

"You will know truth and truth will set you free."
—JOHN 8:32

Today, I continue my work of analysis and introspection to determine the path I want to take and the work that I must do. I believe that I can achieve happiness, so I seek to organize my life accordingly. I analyze my emotional and professional relationships and I identify those who contribute to my happiness and those who are harmful to me. I draw up a plan of action to maintain healthy relationships and to put an end to those who have a negative effect in my life. I look for ways to improve my financial situation and the quality of my day-to-day life. I make a list of the important goals I want to reach during the coming year and in the longer term.

New Year's Resolutions

Many people make New Year's resolutions. They seek to formulate decisions to put an end to old habits, to develop new ones or to achieve objectives that are important to them. Sometimes, we succeed in keeping our resolutions, but often, very early in the New Year, we set aside our good intentions and resume our old habits. The reason is very simple: the decision or resolution has come up against an older resolution or the strong force of our habits.

Before making a resolution, we should evaluate the effort needed to break our old habits and the level of commitment and genuine desire we need to stick to our resolution. Lastly, it is always interesting to identify the circumstances and motivations that incited us to develop the habits or behaviors we now want to change. A bit of groundwork goes a long way.